1991/1992

REEF NOTES
Revisited and Revised
by Julian Sprung

Book Design by Daniel N. Ramirez

Published by Ricordea Publishing Inc.
Coconut Grove, Florida 33133

First Printing May 1996

Published by Ricordea Publishing Inc.
4016 El Prado Blvd.
Coconut Grove, Florida, USA, 33133

To purchase back issues of *Freshwater And Marine Aquarium* magazine or copies of the original "Reef Notes" articles contact: *FAMA*, 144 W. Sierra Madre Blvd., Sierra Madre, CA, 91024

Printed and bound by Arnoldo Mondadori, Verona, Italy.

Design and production by Daniel N. Ramirez
Cover photos by: Daniel N. Ramirez and Julian Sprung.

ISBN 1-883693-23-3

Julian Sprung, 1966 - Reef Notes

This book is dedicated to all the great people I've met at aquarium society shows and conferences, especially the handful of people in each organization who always do the extra work to make everything run smoothly.

Acknowledgments

The following people have contributed to this book either directly or indirectly through their work and exchange of ideas: Dr. Walter Adey, Marj Awai, Stanley Brown, Dr. Robert W. Buddemeier, Roger Bull, John and Patty Burleson, Dr. Bruce Carlson, Merrill Cohen, J. Charles Delbeek, Don Dewey and the Staff at FAMA, Dr. Phillip Dustan, Svein Fosså, Thomas A. Frakes, Bob Goemans, Santiago Guetierrez, Jens Krarup, Brian LaPointe, Karen Loveland, Dr. Frank Maturo, Scott W. Michael, Martin A. Moe, Jr. and Barbara Moe, Alf Jacob Nilsen, Dr. James Norris, Mike Paletta, Daniel and Carmen Ramirez, Eric Sisitsky, Dietrich Stüber and the members of the Berlin Association for Marine Aquaristics, John Tullock, Dr. John Veron, and Peter Wilkens.

Table of Contents

About the Author

Julian Sprung was born in 1966 in Miami Beach, Florida. He is a graduate of the University of Florida with a Bachelor of Science degree in zoology, and is an author, consultant, and frequent lecturer on marine aquarium keeping. He has been keeping marine aquariums for over 18 years, and began studying marinelife more than 20 years ago along the shores of the island where he grew up on Biscayne Bay. Julian writes the monthly column, "Reef Notes" in *Freshwater and Marine Aquarium* magazine, on which this book is based. He has authored numerous articles in other publications such as *Seascope* and *Tropical Fish Hobbyist,* and was Science Editor for the quarterly journal, *Aquarium Frontiers* from 1993-1995. Julian also wrote and produced a video entitled *An Introduction to the Hobby of Reef Keeping.* In 1994 J. Charles Delbeek and Julian Sprung completed over four years of work with the publication of their book *The Reef Aquarium, Vol 1.* As of this printing *The Reef Aquarium, Vol 2* is nearing completion.

Introduction

In volume one I explained that with this series I am enjoying the opportunity to look back at the advice I've given in my columns, offer new suggestions and revise the points where I was in error. By reviewing and revising the columns, I show the progression of opinion regarding the proper ways to manage a reef aquarium.

I am happy with all of the positive feedback regarding the first volume in this series. Clearly there has been a need to get all of these old columns into one place for easy access. Furthermore, the revisions have been helpful. Some of the comments about volume one have been to praise me for being brave enough to criticise my own advice. Actually one could look at it that way or another way: I might just be too vain to leave the imperfect old advice alone when I think it needs to be updated. The way I see it, we are still learning so much about coral reefs and the care of them in closed aquariums that this information evolves. This evolution parallels the reason I gave in the introduction in volume one for why a reef tank inspires so many questions: "The hunger for information seems to be the product of a desire to achieve the perfect aquarium. A perfect reef aquarium is not just another pretty tank. It is a living ecosystem, thriving, growing, and ever-changing with a diverse number of plants and animals that give it stability and beauty. When we strive for perfect balance in a captive ecosystem our endeavor may be akin to trying to manage a small piece of the universe, or the state of our own existence. Aquarists develop an empathy for their aquarium such that they too feel unhealthy when something isn't right with it."

So, one could say I am fiddling with these columns for my own peace of mind as well as the readers. I have always kept the door open to points of view that differ from mine because I feel that the reader should be able to see different perspectives. I have been glad that FAMA editor Don Dewey has promoted this kind of exchange. In "Reef Notes" I encourage techniques that simplify aquarium keeping and improve the environment created. This volume shows the period of transition from tanks with complex life support systems surrounding them to more natural set-ups relying on biology rather than technology. This trend has continued nicely, as you will see in volume three.

Here in volume two we see the beginning of the crave for bigger challenges, such as the small polyped stony corals that build the reef. Another special feature of this volume is the column on lateral line disease. Nowhere else will you find a more thorough coverage of that topic. Other subjects in this volume include how to move a reef tank, lighting options, and of course we pay a visit with the topic of algae control.

We really have come a long way in the seven years since the column began. Nevertheless, I still get some of the same questions from beginning aquarists. I know I've covered all of the common and most of the uncommon lines of inquiry in my columns. Hopefully this book has the answer to your question.

Julian Sprung
February 1996

January 1991

Q. First a note to say how much I do enjoy my subscription to your magazine. Both my sons and I read every issue cover to cover each month. It is by far the "best" aquarium magazine available today!

Between my sons and I, we have 17 freshwater tanks (from 10 gallons to 125 gallons) and four saltwater tanks (55, 70, 95, and 220 gallons). We have been doing well with all, until lately when a problem came up with the 220 gallon tank which we have been unable to identify. I hope you can give me some help, as I am stumped and none of the local dealers or pet shops have been able to come up with an answer. Here is the problem.

The 220 gallon tank has been set up for approximately 15 months and all existing fish and inverts are still doing fine. However, over the last two months, any new fish added to the system die within two to three days. In almost all the cases the fish appear to be okay until death occurs. There is no visible sign of stress and they all appear to eat well. The types of fish added and lost in the last two months were: Moorish Idols, Yellow Tangs, Percula Clowns, Tomato Clowns, Flame Angel, Queen Angel, and Christmas wrasse. The fish were generally added two at a time, several weeks apart. I have tried isolation in a hospital tank for two weeks before adding to the 220 gallon tank, but still experience the same loss factor. I have tried rearranging the entire tank when adding new fish, so that there is no stress from the other fish defending any area, and I have run tests for pH, salinity, nitrite, nitrate, ammonia, etc. Still no answer. I went from one water change of 25% per month, to one 25% water change every weekend for the last month and a half. Still the new fish die, and the old fish and inverts are fine. Please note that some of the new fish added are the same type that are already in the tank, such as Percula clown, and yet only the new ones die. None of the dead fish or existing live fish show any outward signs of damage or sickness.

Listed below is the tank data:
Size: 220 gallon, all glass. Set up approximately 15 months ago, trouble started approximately two months ago. Filtration: Trickle filter with DLS and drip plate, and

two Magnum® 330 filled with Chemi-Pure®.
Two powerheads in the tank for circulation.
Three electronic heaters 250 watts, set and maintained at
78°. Specific gravity: 1.022, ammonia: 0, nitrite: 0, nitrate:
10ppm, pH: 8.0. Tests done with Sea-Test® kit.
Existing and growing in the tank: one Percula Clown 1
1/2"; two Blue Damsels 1 1/2"; one Fox Face 5"; one
Dragon Wrasse 4"; one Maroon Clown 3"; one Velvet
damsel 4"; two Striper Damsels; eight Turbo Grazer
snails-1 1/2"; one Long spine urchin; two small
Mushroom rocks 5"; one Purple anemone; one Bubble
coral 5"; five Curley-Cue anemones; two Yellow
anemones; one Skunk Cleaner shrimp, and 60 lbs. of live
rock. There are also four pieces of bleached coral.
Approximately 2" crushed coral base. 620 watts white
Actinic 03 lighting on 12 hours a day. Feeding: frozen
food, Formula 1 & 2 each morning, live food, worms or
brine shrimp each evening. I am very desperate for an
answer, please help if you can. Sincerely, Phil
Czajkowski, Geneva, lllinois

A. Thanks for the compliments, Phil, and thanks for
going to the trouble to provide many details of information which help me eliminate certain possibilities and
suspect others. Many hobbyists that I have spoken to
have discussed a similar problem with adding new fish
to an established reef tank only their losses are attributed
to disease. The problem is similar in that old residents
remain healthy, while new additions quickly succumb
and die. . . not so quick as yours, however, and your
confidence about their undamaged appearance makes
me reasonably confident that disease is not the factor in
your troublesome set-up. Nevertheless, I want to take
the opportunity to address the disease problem as it is a
common occurrence. While the outbreak of white spot,
Cryptocaryon may occur on occasion, in a reef tank it
usually subsides providing the temperature is maintained
constant. In contrast, the other "white spot" disease,
Amyloodinium does not subside so easily, and may
slowly wipe out the entire fish population. The only recommendation I can give when the plague hits a reef tank
full of invertebrates is to lower the specific gravity to
about 1.017 over a period of days, not lowering it more
than .003 per day. When lowering the specific gravity

one may need to boost the calcium level in the aquarium. Make sure to maintain a carbonate hardness of at least 8 degrees, and a calcium level of 400 mg/L or higher. This will help your invertebrates and plants adapt to the lower specific gravity. Do not add any new fish to the tank until all symptoms have disappeared from all fish for at least three weeks. Sometimes the old residents remain without symptoms, as they have built up an immunity, but new additions quickly succumb to the disease. Sometimes old residents succumb and die as well, and this can usually be attributed to nutritional deficiency weakening the fish's immunity. I will have more to say about disease, nutrition, and immunity soon.

I have some comments to make about your attempted additions. Regarding the Moorish idols and Yellow tangs, all tangs are very prone to *Cryptocaryon* and *Amyloodinium*, and they should be quarantined with copper sulfate before adding to the reef tank. Of course one can always "get away with it," but there are risks involved. Yellow tangs also carry black spot disease, a turbellarian parasite which usually goes away on its own in a reef tank, but which can cause "difficult to control" fish loss. Formalin baths during the quarantine procedure take care of black spot. Percula and Tomato Clowns often succumb to a white slime disease which I described last month. Please read the recommended treatment for this problem. If you already have one established Percula Clown in the tank, as you do Phil, it is best to add only a very small specimen. Clownfish are born males and become females*. Therefore, you are most likely to obtain a pair in your circumstance by adding a small clown. Flame angels are very susceptible to *Amyloodinium*, in my experience, but are generally, though not always, good fish in the reef tank**. The Queen angel, however, is seldom a good addition to a reef tank. Most will devour your prized invertebrates.

Now I have some comments to make about some of your present tank inhabitants. A four inch Velvet Damsel is a mean customer, even in a 220 gallon tank. The Maroon Clown as well, at three inches, might not take kindly to new additions to her territory. Come to think of it, you have a lot of Damsels there. Still, you say that the

---

*Actually clownfish are born sexually immature of course. As they mature they become male first then female. The largest individual in a group of clownfish living in the same anemone is the female. One of the next largest is her mate. The remaining fish are potential mates. If the female dies, the dominant male that is her mate becomes a female.

**I don't recommend Flame angels for most reef aquariums either as they have a "sweet tooth" for coral and giant clams too. In general all angelfish except *Genicanthus* species are potential coral and/or clam eaters. The damage is done primarily to fleshy stony corals and soft corals. In reef tanks composed of small polyped stony corals, angelfish can be maintained safely in the same aquarium, but beware of their impact on the giant clams!

dead fish show no signs of damage, so I will assume that they are not getting beat up. You have five Curley-Cue anemones. Assuming you are not confusing them with diminutive *Aiptasia* anemones, the curley-cues, which may have tentacles spanning over a foot, are really bad about stinging fish and invertebrates. I would never put a Moorish Idol in a tank with curley-cue anemones. Don't get me wrong, Curley-Cues are fascinating and beautiful, but they are also not very desirable with respect to the rest of the community.

I bring up these comments because it has been my experience that although there may be one main factor causing a problem, there are also numerous other peripheral factors which may have played a role in the loss of specific specimens. Diagnosing problems by mail, as I do, is both difficult and irresponsible. So to gain any sense of responsibility I must try to cover all bases.

With that said, I will now tell you what I think is causing the loss of new additions to your tank. You said it — a two inch gravel base. Under certain strong water flow conditions this would be no problem, though the tank would be better off with a thinner layer or none at all*. . . I understand the requirement for the wrasses. I suspect that the circulation in your tank is not adequate enough to prevent this gravel bed from becoming anaerobic, and that the dissolved oxygen level in the tank is falling so low at night that the new fish are simply suffocating. When fish asphyxiate like this, they typically die with their gills flared wide open. . . the look is unmistakable. Your resident fish may have adapted to the lower oxygen levels through changes in their blood. You didn't mention whether there is gravel in the wet section of your filter. If there is this would only worsen the problem.

So, what to do? Well, first of all, if it is possible to maintain the same stability at a lower temperature, like 74° instead of 78° for instance, it would significantly raise the level of oxygen that could dissolve in the water. Of course I'm going to tell you to remove most of the gravel from the tank, and all of it from the wet filter if it is there. If you have no problem with taking the reef apart, as you

*Nowadays we are using gravel beds of even more than two inches, but incorporated with a plenum below. Please refer to volume one of this series for a complete description of Jaubert's system. I still agree with my suspicion in this example that anaerobic pockets in Mr. Czajkowski's gravel suffocated the new fish. In addition to low oxygen, toxic hydrogen sulfide that can be produced under anaerobic conditions might also have suffocated the fish.

indicated, I suggest that you remove the rocks and set them aside (not in the sun or heat !), remove the fish and place them in several large, lidded, aerated containers filled with water from the aquarium, and siphon out all of the gravel into another large container. This procedure will probably waste about 25% of the water, so you will be making the usual water change. Then reassemble the reef on the bare bottom, making sure the structure is loose enough to allow access to the back for siphoning out detritus. I guarantee you the gravel is dirty ! For the benefit of the wrasse and any future wrasses, you may add one inch of the old gravel, which you have thoroughly rinsed in aquarium water, to the front of the reef. Finally, you might consider removing the Velvet damsel or any other particularly aggressive pets, and the fate of your curley-cues is up to you, but remember my warning. These changes should solve your difficulty with new fish. Hey, holding the fish for two weeks prior to adding them to the tank is a good idea.

Febuary 1991

Recently I returned from another visit with the fishy folks up in Toronto where, in a lecture I commented that a successful reef aquarium is about ten percent the product of the equipment utilized and about ninety percent a product of the aquarist's "finesse." This month is a real treat as we finally begin to see some nice pictures of reef aquaria maintained under different regimes by DIFFERENT PEOPLE. To get a completely honest demonstration of the difference that results from the use of different types of equipment, we would need to see aquaria set up and maintained by the same person. Nevertheless, these photographs and others I intend to have in this column periodically, will afford some sense of the extent of the difference between aquaria, and a sense that perhaps this difference has something to do with the equipment used and how the aquarium is maintained. Seeing a variety of successful aquaria helps the aquarist make decisions about what his or her goals are in this hobby. Would that we could see them all at once, but one or two at a time is the best I can do. First, the questions.

Q. I am writing this letter to express my feelings about marine aquariums. I don't know why people say that they are alot of work. I have maintained a 55 gallon

marine aquarium for six months with two clowns
Amphiprion percula, a scribbled angel *Chaetodontoplus duboulayi*, a Dragon Wrasse *Novaculichthys taeniourus*, a batfish *Platax orbicularis*, a Blue Head Butterfly *Chaetodon kleini*, and a Cleaner Wrasse *Labroides dimidiatus*. I had a few small problems in the beginning that were easily solved. My aquarium has been quite easy to maintain, and I have had no trouble keeping up with the monthly water changes and feeding my fish. Perhaps you should know that I use a wet/dry filter and that I am 12 years old. So my advice to future marine aquarists is to not let anyone talk you out of it and if you really want a marine aquarium don't give up!
Lucas Alonso, Largo, Fl.

A. No question there... thank you Lucas.

Q. What can you tell us about the use of potassium per-manganate for water quality improvement? I know a little about the misuses. I recently bought some at a drugstore and proceeded to put a very small quantity into my tank. The redox shot up from about 315 to 465 in about fifteen seconds. Oops! Needless to say, the inverts didn't like it. But then these corals have a way of surviving the most foolish of mistakes their owners make. Everything did! Future doses of great dilution does improve redox. What is known about this?

A. While it is known that certain oxidizing solutions such as potassium permanganate and hydrogen peroxide can rapidly elevate the redox potential value of the aquarium water, I do not recommend the practice of adding these solutions to the aquarium, even in a con-trolled manner. There is room for careful experimenta-tion and exploration with our aquaria, of course, but the witchcraft approach of adding magic potions to improve the aquarium is beyond foolish. Please refrain from adding the potassium permanganate, and concentrate on proper maintenance procedures to keep the redox high. In response to my recommendation here, I anticipate some readers telling me of some beneficial experiences with redox raising solutions. One must understand that when I give this advice, my position necessitates that I offer a warning about practices which might be risky or endanger the lives of our little captive reefs. One might question the difference between my recommendations concerning the addition of potassium permanganate and say, a "trace element" such as Strontium or Iodine. To this I can only answer that the latter two have been demonstrated to be directly utilized by the invertebrates and plants, both in the scientific and aquarium literature. I intend to discuss the subject of trace element additions in detail in a future column as I have been observing some very exciting results.

Q. Dear Julian

Over the past five months I've been slowly setting up a 70 gallon reef system. On August 31st I put 79 lbs. of cured, base live rock into the tank and began cycling it. On September 28th I added 84 lbs of cured live rock evenly split between base rock and plant rock. Each time I spent about 2 and 1/2 hours going over the rock removing any hitchhikers, before rinsing it in salt water and putting it into the tank. Except for one piece of red algae rock (Rhodophyceae) and four Turbo snails nothing else has been added.

To my chagrin, two days after the last batch of rock, I found one bristle worm, which I immediately removed with a tweezers, and one inch to inch and a half long mantis shrimp (*Squilla empusa*), identified using Moe's Marine Aquarium Reference. I removed the rock I first saw him scurrying around and probed it with a steel dental pick but found nothing. On several occasions I've gotten up in the middle of the night in hopes of finding him and where he hides but all I've found is one more bristle worm. I've searched just after the HQI lamps go out and just before they come on, when only the actinics are on, again to no avail. I've even considered taking all the rock out and reinspecting each piece but doubt the utility of this method, since I failed to find him the first time.

Two days after noticing the mantis shrimp I discovered two other shrimp about 3/4 inch in length, narrow, with long antennae and under the HQI/Actinic lighting they seemed translucent. Ten days later I observed about a dozen 1/4 inch shrimp that I can't identify. I'm not convinced they aren't mantis shrimp. They lack the extend-

ed eye sockets visible on the adult, but have large che-
lipeds that are kept tucked in under the cephalothorax
and thrust out laterally as they play.

After reviewing available past issues of FAMA and the
books I have on hand I could only find suggestions on
removing bristle worms. I would appreciate any suggestions you can provide on removing this menace and
identifying juvenile mantis shrimp, since I do not want a
tank devoted to mantis shrimp. Sincerely, Melvin J.
Williams, Jr., Uncasville, Ct.

A.. Nuke 'em. Somehow you missed my suggestions
concerning mantis shrimp in the particularly informative
"REEF NOTES" in the June 1989 issue of "FAMA." I will
not repeat them. If you want to see the beast(s) I suggest you refrain from feeding the tank for about a week,
then watch the tank when you do finally put some food
in. The smell of food usually brings them out.

The 3/4 inch shrimp with long antennae are probably
pistol shrimps, *Alpheus* or *Synalpheus* sp. These make a
percussion concussion clicking sound that is similar to
that of the mantis shrimp, but they are generally not as
dangerous, so don't worry about 'em. In Europe, pistol
shrimps are intentionally added to reef tanks which have
sand on the bottom, in order to make use of their habit
of constantly stirring and sifting the substrate. They also
make natural and fascinating partnerships with the various "sleeper gobies" which also burrow in the sand.

The 1/4 inch "shrimp" which you suspected were baby
stomatopods are probably Amphipods, highly desirable,
mostly herbivorous crustaceans which feed on undesirable algae, detritus, and uneaten food. They are terrific
live food for the fish...sea horses and mandarins love
them.

One last thing... "Cured" rock by definition is "cycled,"
though there is certainly nothing wrong with being
patient and allowing plenty of time between putting the
rock in and stocking with specimens. The longer you
wait, the better the chance you will develop sustainable

populations of such desirable critters as the amphipods and copepods. Sounds like your tank is coming along nicely.

Now it's time to begin the tour of the tanks!

Thiel Aqua Tech reef, photos by Albert Thiel:
Photo #1 shows a *Euphyllia ancora*, "Hammer coral"
Photo #2 shows some *Actinodiscus* mushroom anemones.

Julian,
In a recent article you asked for photographs illustrating the use of metal halide lighting over a reef home type aquarium.

Here are a few. I am not the best of photographers, so please forgive the quality of some.

Tank Data:
Size: 135 gallons, plus sump: 18 gallons, Total size: 153 gallons, Displacement by rocks, tested by placing the rocks in a vat of known content, and letting it overflow. Remove rocks. Measure what's left.= 22 gallons
Net gallonage of system: 131.00 gallons.Redox potential 7:00 a.m. in sump: 464 mv, in tank: 412 mv. Noon in sump: 449 mv, in tank: 396 mv. Ozone and a redox potential controller are used. Brand: ours. Dissolved oxygen (in tank) 7:00 am 9+ mg/L, noon: 10+mg/L, 8:00 pm: 9+ mg/L, a pressurized oxygen rector running at 5psi is used 24 hours a day, injected regular air. Nitrate measured as $N-NO_3$, 0.2ppm, Phosphate measured as Ortho PO_4, 0.01ppm, Test kits used are by Lamotte chemicals (low range tests). Lighting is by 4 (four) 175 watt 5500 K metal halides Coralife brand, placed 14 inches (bulb) from the water surface.

Photoperiod is as follows:
175 watt for a full 14 hours
350 watt for a full 10 hours
525 watt for a full 7 hours
700 watt for a full 4 hours (from 11 am to 3 pm)
Staggering of lighting is done by an electronic timer.
Additives used: KSM (strontium + molybdenum supplement)
Liquid Gold (micro-nutrient supplement)

Trace elements: Vitamins (to food only) We use a mixture of Hawaiian Marinemix and Tech Reef Salt. Automatic water changer changes 1.5 gallons per day, at 8:00 am, Feeding is light. Brachionus are added once a month. Filtration is then stopped completely for a total of 90 minutes. Filtration: Platinum 15 gallon filter with 15 gallons of balls. Venturi protein skimmer (our brand) with molded venturi valve. Chemical filtration by means of Poly Bio Marine molecular absorption discs (24) X-Nitrate and X-Phosphate compounds are used to keep the nitrates and phosphates low. Mechanical filtration is by means of a foam fine filter attached to the pump intakes, and cleaned once a week. A small amount of carbon is placed where the water from the skimmer remixes with the sump's water to remove any residual ozone (vegetable based carbon is used). If you have any questions please call me. Regards, Albert J. Thiel

Anthony D. Vaccarello's reef: Photo #3 shows an overall view of Mr. Vaccarello's aquarium, including a large "centerpiece" *Sarcophyton glaucum*, a triple header colony of *Sarcophyton trocheliophorum*, an elegance coral far left, *Cladiella* "colt" coral*, upper right corner, two Sinularia species, to the left of the colt coral, a couple of Tridacna derasa clams, various plants including *Caulerpa, Dictyosphaerium, Padina, Sargassum,* and *Dasycladus,* mushroom anemones, yellow polyp, *Xenia* above and to the left of clam, star polyp, and a long-tentacle anemone. One can see that the reef is suspended on cut sections of pvc pipe.

*Colt coral is *Alcyonium,* not *Cladiella.*

Dear Mr. Julian,
First I would like to say how much I enjoy reading your column. It is one of my favorite sections in FAMA. I enjoy reading the questions that other people ask and find the information that you provide very useful.
I have enclosed pictures of my 55 gallon reef aquarium. The aquarium has been established for over eight months now. I know you are familiar with Mike Paletta's reef system. Mike was very helpful to me in establishing my reef aquarium. Most of the invertebrates in my reef have been purchased from eastern Pennsylvania on some of the trips I have taken with Mike. Hopefully over time, I can be of some help to the aquarium hobby

Photo: 1

Photo: 2

Photo: 3

when it comes to providing observations and information as to what works and what doesn't work so well in a reef aquarium.

My reef includes several different kinds of finger corals, leather corals, *Zoanthus, Xenia,* mushroom rock, anemone rock, feather dusters, hermit crabs, cleaner shrimp along with an Elegance Coral, Open Brain, Bubble Coral and *Tridacna* clams.

The fish are currently limited to a Flame Angel, Yellow Tang and a seven line wrasse. Equipment includes a wet/dry filter, a homemade oxygen rector, Tunze skimmer, Tunze redox controller, ozonizer (used in conjunction with the redox controller), air dryer, power heads controlled by a time phased delay relay to provide alternating currents and six 40 watt fluorescent lamps: two actinic, two ultralumes and two daylights. I measure the redox from the sump of the wet/dry filter and it is maintained around 460 at night and 440 during the day. I also change the prefilter material every other day, siphon detritus from the bottom weekly, and perform a 10% water change every two weeks.

The light combination seems to be working quite well. Many of the anemones I have purchased were white in color. After placing them in the tank, they have turned brown in color. Also, a small *Tridacna* clam that I purchased was very pale in color. After a period of time in my tank, it now contains some very nice vivid coloration. I feel that this is a good indication that the zooxanthellae is doing very well in the invertebrates. Most of the mushroom rock and *Zoanthus* has reproduced. The clams and especially the soft corals have grown in size. Thank you for your time and contributions to the field of reef aquariums. Anthony D. Vaccarello, Allison Park, P.A.

Thanks to everyone for sending in the photos and info on the aquaria...I've suddenly been getting heaps of pix from you! I hope that this month's column has inspired some of you, and I hope that you keep on sending me pictures as I intend to keep on featuring Hobbyists' reef tanks periodically.

March 1991

Let's start out this month's column with a tune that I know all you reef keeping fanatics can appreciate, especially as a reminder why you should never put your hand in the tank late at night, or for something you think will "only take a minute."

Sung to the tune of Tom Petty's recent hit "Free Falling"

> Got a reef-tank,
> It looks really fine,
> It's got wet/dry,
> venturi skimmer too.
> But there's one piece,
> just doesn't look right,
> Gotta move it...just a little to the right,
>
> Now my reef, my reef's falling
> (Reef's falling, now my reef's falling, now my...)
> - Guitar solo-

Note: **The use of underwater epoxy, plastic cable ties, and plastic screws or rods can provide a more stable structure and prevent reef collapses.**

And while we're on the subject of reef's falling...

I received a letter in answer to my request for information about designs to prevent damage or loss to the home and aquarium in the event of an earthquake, and would like to share the information with you.

Q. Dear Julian:
This is in reference to your November article in FAMA, and the reader who wanted some information on earthquake damage prevention to larger aquariums.

The essence is to limit the amount of vibration delivered to the aquarium - this can be done, as the architect indicated, by providing a shock-absorbing system to the aquarium base. A better method would be to provide an isolated base to begin with that the aquarium or its cabinet rests on. these isolated bases are part of every good vibration-reduction design in buildings housing large generators.

One step further would be to provide such a base but construct it as a confined compressible medium "like quicksand," etc. The theory here is that upon mass vibration and tilting of the house, the fluid nature of the confined medium would allow its surrounding housing to move, but itself and what is above it (the aquarium) would remain relatively motionless.

Please refer to the following simple diagram depicting the kind of isolation base being discussed.

Once you know the theory, the next step is to have an engineer you may know do a few simple calculations. Then you will have a materials list and some money to pay out. If you are a handyman to begin with, the solution may not be all that expensive.

Good luck to your reader. I hope he is able to make use of this info.With kind regards, Frank G. Anderson, Saudi Arabia

A. Thank you very much, Frank! I really appreciate the reply.

...another letter in one of those funny red, white, and blue striped envelopes... Oh, and listen up, this one's for "freshwater people"

Q. Dear Sir, I have a 100 gallon tropical tank. Filtration is by two Eheim thermofilters, with Siporax. I also have separate undergravel heating and a semi-automatic CO_2 system which maintains the pH around 7. The water is soft at about 3-4 degrees hardness, as all water here is very soft. The tank is lit 10 hours/day by two metal halide lights.

Several weeks ago I stripped the tank down and bleached it to cure an algae problem. Unfortunately, despite very heavy planting, the algae has returned. It is a short bearded brush algae, about 5mm long, and dark grey in colour. I do believe it may be part of the red algae group. I have treated the tank with a mixture of Wardley's all clear tablets, and Hobby Algen killer with little success. I would be greatful for any suggestions before it overwhelms my tank again. Bleaching the whole thing again just isn't on.

Thank you for your kind attention and I look forward to

Frank G. Anderson's suggested way to build a supporting structure to prevent earthquake damage to an aquarium.

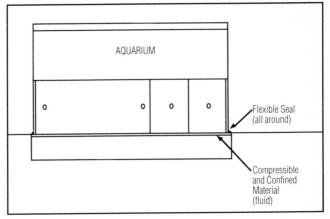

hearing from you. Yours faithfully, Philip Lockie, Belfast, U.K.

A. Naturally the answer to this question applies both to fresh and sea water aquariums, so don't you old salts skim by this one too quickly. What we have here is a hobbyist with a good system... more sophisticated than most, being misled by bad advice from someone, and not having a thorough grasp on the ecological balance of the aquarium and how it relates to the technical gadgetry in use. The high intensity lights are ideal for making the plants grow, but in the presence of excessive plant nutrients (phosphorous and nitrogen), these lights will likewise be ideal for the explosive growth of algae. The CO_2 used also benefits both the desirable plants and the undesirable algae. The problem, then, is a source of too much plant nutrients. In your letter you did not indicate how many of what kind of fish this aquarium contains. The fish population and the quantity of food you feed them relates to the amount of plant nutrients available to the plants and algae. I suspect that fish are not your problem, though certain species definitely are part of the cure, as I will describe in a moment. Most likely the source of your frustration is the water in your area. As you replenish water lost to evaporation, or make a partial water change, you are feeding the algae. I have covered this subject numerous times in this column as it relates to the control of undesirable algae in tropical reef aquaria. The solution, in part, is to use water that is free from plant nutrients, via reverse osmosis and/or deionization. In addition, it is good practice to have plenty of algae grazing herbivores. About ten to twenty small *Ottocinclus affenis* would be most useful in preventing the growth of the brush algae in your aquarium. You might also employ one or more *Epalzeorhinchus siamensis*, though you might not like their disposition as they grow larger. The herbivores you choose should graze the algae off of the leaves, but not actually graze the leaves themselves, much as the marine "Tangs" of the genus *Ctenochaetus* simply "kiss" the diatoms off of a blade of Caulerpa without doing any harm. Many of the herbivorous snails in freshwater will damage the plants in addition to eating the algae, but there are some which do not do any harm.

Do not listen to whoever is advising you to add algicides or to strip clean your tank. By all means continue with your system, but with make-up water free from algae nutrients, and yes do continue with the dense-planting approach. If you have been advised to use some kind of fertilizing concoction in addition, be sure that it is merely iron and or a vitamin/trace element mixture, not containing phosphate or nitrate.

Finally, should there still be a chronic appearance of brush algae despite the herbivores and nutrient free water, you might consider shortening the photoperiod from 10 hours to 7 or 8 instead. Alternately, you might add a couple of fluorescents as viewing light, while only employing the metal halides for 4 to 6 hours during the day, thereby still having the total ten hour photoperiod so you can enjoy the aquarium in the evenings when you are home.

Thanks for your letter! One last thing, if you don't already have a copy, do please read *The Optimum Aquarium* by Kaspar Horst and Horst Kipper. It thoroughly covers all aspects of the equipment you are using and the essential parameters of a successful planted aquarium.

I have received a number of letters all essentially from hobbyists concerned about a chronic problem with "ICH" (*Cryptocaryon*) in their reef aquarium. While I have covered this one before, I'll briefly state again what I do to remedy this situation:

1. Stabilize the temperature...no fluctuations beyond ± 1°.
2. Lower the specific gravity to 1.020 while maintaining the calcium level above 400 mg/l via the addition of calcium chloride. I have experienced no deleterious effects in reef aquaria even at 1.017 s.g., as long as the calcium level is maintained.*

*It is also critical that the alkalinity be elevated when diluting the salinity. Please see volume one of this series for a thorough explanation.

This method is very effective in preventing losses to *Cryptocaryon*, but unfortunately is less effective against *Amyloodinium*. Of course it is always wise to quarantine all fishes, especially if you really wish to keep them alive.

Now we continue with some more of your reef aquarium photos accompanied by system description.

Aquarium number one: John Burleson's reef.

Photo #1 shows two fully expanded leather corals (*Sarcophyton trocheliophorum*) along with Green star Polyp (*Clavularia viridis***), and an *Anthelia* sp. below it. In the bottom right corner is part of the "mantle" of a giant clam, *Tridacna squamosa*, and also visible are various mushroom anemones, *Ricordea florida* and *Actinodiscus* sp, part of an elegance coral, *Catalaphyllia jardinei*, yellow polyps, *Parazoanthus* sp., a small "giant clam", *T. crocea* or *T. maxima* upper right, and *Nepthea* sp. in the lower left corner. Photo #2 shows a "bed" of mushroom anemones, *Actinodiscus* sp. The photos were taken with a 35 mm Minolta using Kodac VRG Gold 200 film.

**Green Star Polyp in this case is probably a *Briareum* sp. Brown Star Polyp, which can also be green in color, is *Pachyclavularia violacea*. The photo is cropped here and in the original column so some creatures mentioned are not visible.

The system:

Two corner overflows feed surface water to a Pisces 1000 wet/dry filter with two 3/4 inch rotating spraybars and Dupla bioball media. The return pump is an Iwaki MD 70RLT. 15 mg per hour of ozone is pumped into the Pisces filter's protein skimmer, which is thus used for ozone contact only. A Tunze centifugal protein skimmer with venturi air injection and protein concentration gradient uptake grid is mounted separately, and takes water directly from the tank so it is not affected by the ozone used in the Pisces filter. The direction of water flow in the aquarium changes at regular intervals, owing

Photo: 1

Photo: 2

to the use of two returns and two 3/4 inch Electromini ball valves made by Asahi, with a digital Omron timer used for sequencing. The valves switch every 370 minutes. Automatic water make-up for evaporation is handled by means of an infra-red level-sensing device that powers a dosing pump when a drop in the sump level is detected. Make up water is filtered through a reverse osmosis unit and a deionization unit, and is then stored in a closed drum.

Calcium chloride is added to the aquarium periodically to maintain a calcium level of 470 mg/L. The carbonate hardness is maintained at 9 dkh by the occasional addition of a marine buffer. A Dupla CO_2 injection system is also in use to maintain a maximum pH of 8.3. The Nitrate level is .2 ppm. No denitrifying filter is used. Both inorganic and organic phosphate levels in the water are 0 ppm (Hach test kit). The temperature is kept at 76 degrees with a chiller, and the specific gravity is kept at 1.023. H.W. Marinemix salt is used. Dupla carbon is used in the sump of the filter.

The lighting:

Lighting is accomplished with six VHO fluorescent tubes. Three are 5 foot 140watt Philips Actinics, and the other three are 6 foot 160 watt Sylvania Daylights. No lenses or sleeves are used between the tank surface and the bulbs. The lights are staggered by timers to simulate the change in intensity during the day.

The light schedule is as follows: At 8:00 A.M. two of the daylights come on, then at 10:00 A.M. two of the Actinics come on. At noon the remaining Actinic and remaining Daylight come on, and these two bulbs stay on until 4:00 P.M. The other two Daylight bulbs are turned off at 6:00 P.M., and the other two Actinic bulbs are turned off at 8:00 P.M.

E.J. Howard's Reef:

Photo #3 shows a view of a portion of Mr. Howard's tank, with a Flame Angel, Copperband Butterfly, and two Ocellaris Clowns. Hard corals include an Open Brain Coral, *Trachyphyllia geofroyi*, above and to the left of center, a *Tubastraea* coral above it, an Elegance Coral, *Catalaphyllia*, tentacles barely visible lower left. A Hammer Coral, *Euphyllia ancora*, tentacles barely visible upper right, some mushroom anemones, some yellow polyp, a carpet anemone lower right, and Star Polyp below and to the left of the open brain coral.

Photo #4 shows a nice hard coral, *Turbinaria peltata*

Equipment:

100 gallon glass tank, 20 gallon trickle filter, Sanders protein skimmer, Sanders model 100 ozone generator (nor-

Photo: 3

Photo: 4

mally runs at 50%, and return water is run through coconut shell carbon) Thiel Aqua Tech Air Dryer and Filter, 4 power heads (2 Aquaclear 800, 2 Visi-jet 100) These are controlled by a Thiel Aqua Tech ocean motion device, Thiel Aqua Tech X-Nitrate.

The tank has been running for approx. four years with no major problems, knock on wood. I use Reef Care Invert. Feeder Blocks, T.A.T. Tech Vita Trace Complex, T.A.T. Tech Reef Elements, Assorted Coralife foods, Live brine, frozen shrimp, and squid.

Lighting:
Energy Savers Metal Hood with fan and lens between
bulbs and tank.

The hood is suspended six inches above the water, and
has two Coralife 5500 K metal halide bulbs, and two
Triton 40 watt fluorescents.

Timing:
First Triton on at 7:30 a.m., second Triton on at 9:00 a.m.,
Metal Halides on at 10:30 a.m. Metal Halides off at 7:30
p.m. Second Triton off at 9:00 p.m. First Triton off at 10:30
p.m. Fifteen hours of total light. Nine hours of peak light.
The tank receives no natural light at all. E.J. Howard,
Slidell, La.

Thanks for the photo's, there's plenty more of them. Stay
tuned folks as next month I might finally get around to
talking about trace compound additions as I've
promised. Till then, just think, as I write it is December
and a chilly 75 degrees outside...if the weather were better and I could just find the time, I'd be on a reef.

May 1991

I hope everyone is enjoying the views of hobbyist's reef
tanks. Maybe now you're saying, "Hey, my reef looks
better than those." Perhaps you've picked up some useful tips that will help yours look better. This month I'm
answering some more letters, and leaving the show of
reef tanks for the next column...I have a nice one from
Australia to show you.

Darn, I just looked back at last month's column and saw
that I promised to talk about trace element additions.
Promises, promises. I'd rather just answer a few questions. Well alright, I'll talk about one that I feel confident
will make a BIG difference in your reef tank, strontium
chloride. Strontium additions have been discussed by
numerous aquarium authors, Wilkens, Thiel, Nilsen,
Delbeek, and Stüber, to name a few. The purpose of
adding strontium is to assist in the calcification processes
of corals and calcareous algae. While some of these actually incorporate the strontium in their skeletons, the
function of strontium appears to be more as an assist to
the passage of calcium across the cell membrane. The

exact mechanism by which strontium assists this calcium extraction from the water is not known. Nevertheless, the benefit of adding it to an aquarium can be seen in the increase in stony coral growth and especially in the explosive increase in coralline algae growth. The pink and purple encrusting circular plates of coralline algae spreading on the rocks and glass really enhance the beauty and natural look of the aquarium, and in turn impede the growth of undesirable algae like *Derbesia*. Some of the soft corals such as gorgonians and star polyps, which have calcareous spicules embedded in their tissues, also show increases in growth with strontium additions. It is important to note, however, that calcium levels in the aquarium will fall as a result of the enhanced growth stimulated by the strontium, and that calcium additions are ultimately necessary to fully appreciate the benefit of the strontium. Please see the reference list regarding calcium additions.

Strontium chloride stock solution is prepared by dissolving 50 grams of strontium chloride in 500ml. (half a liter) of pure water. This makes a ten percent solution. The dosage is two ml. of this solution per 25 gallons per two weeks. It is best to add it daily, so divide the full dosage by 14. In smaller aquariums this works out to a very minute amount, so the stock may need to be further diluted to obtain practical quantities to add. The strontium chloride comes as a white powder*, and may be obtained from chemical or pharmaceutical companies. Very little is needed, so the slightly high cost can be off-set by inviting your fellow aquarists to "chip in" and buy the strontium together.

*Actually it is more like sugar cystals.

In the future I will discuss other useful trace elements. For now I am providing a brief reference list for your reading pleasure and information at the end of this column. In a recent phone conversation with Peter Wilkens, I learned that he is adding Lithium and Barium to his reef tank, primarily for the benefit of numerous species of *Acropora* corals which he is growing...If I can get a photo you'll soon see. In the references at the end of this column you will find some support for these additions. In future columns I will discuss Lithium, Barium, Boron, and Iodine. Not to worry folks, you are not "falling behind." These elements don't make or break a reef tank...their effect is more subtle, though, as I indicated, strontium's effect is quite remarkable.

Let's look at a few letters I have received somewhat recently.

Q. I'd appreciate some help on marine aquarium Nitrates.

I've had a 52 gallon Salt tank set up for over a year equipped with U.G. filter, two 200-size powerheads with crushed coral and shells. I have a UV, C/C protein skimmer with Tetra® luft pump, Magnum® 330 cannister w/ Chemi-Pure®, Whisper® pump w/ bubble wands. Ammonia, Nitrite, and pH are fine. All equipment is maintained as required.

Fish consist of 2 Green Chromis, a Percula Clown, a Cleaner Wrasse, Pajama Cardinal, Mandarin, Australian Dottyback, and a large 5-6 inch Racoon Butterfly. Newest fish is the dottyback (one month). All others have been in the tank at least 6 months. I've always added weekly doses of Vita-Chem®. I've recently started monthly Reef Care® Vit &Min blocks (My problem, however, existed before these blocks).

My problem is this: I don't believe it's overcrowded, and I think I've the necessary equipment, but my nitrates have increased steadily to 60ppm—I'd prefer to keep it 40 ppm or under. Newly mixed water tests nitrate free- so I'm not starting out high. Back when the tank became established and began building up nitrates, I started with monthly water changes of 10 gallons. Concerned that the substrate would pack down because of powerhead use, I started using a siphon and thoroughly cleaned 1/2 of the bottom (so I wouldn't destroy too many bacteria at once) when changing the water. Since this didn't lower nitrates, I tried siphoning one side with a 4 gallon change, then two weeks later doing a 10 gallon & siphoning the other side. This also made no appreciable difference, so I currently siphon 1/2 the bottom with a 10 gallon change every 3 weeks.

When I feed, no food stays on the bottom. I get a reasonable algae covering on the dead corals and substrate between siphons. Am I creating a problem by rotating the bottom and therefore burying some of the algae-coated particles?

What am I doing wrong? Overfeeding, too much bottom siphoning? Too many vitamin additives? Or should I change more than 10 gallons at a time? I'm confused. Thank you for any information you can give me to put me on the right track. Jackie Krenkel, Chicago Heights, IL

A. Sure, Jackie. First I want to point out that the "problem" concerning you appears to be more a problem in theory rather than a problem in reality...ie. you didn't mention any loss or illness of the specimens you keep, only that the numbers bothered you. Of course the first analogy that comes to mind then is, "If it ain't broke, don't fix it." Nevertheless, you have a valid question which deserves a good answer, certainly better than "Don't worry about it," so I will give you an answer.

Ah, wait. Before I outline some useful steps you might take to help get the situation under your control, Jackie, I want to remind everyone again that it should be the ultimate goal of your endeavor in this aquarium hobby to have a successful tank, and that this success should be based upon the health and beauty of the inhabitants inside the tank environment, not on the numbers or readings of test kits and meters outside of the environment. These gauges have their purpose and utility, but an affect on our happiness with the display is not their function.

Regarding the vitamin additions, It is my opinion that these should be made directly to the food, not the water of the aquarium. Vitamins are co-enzymes which aid in the breakdown and use of the nutritional value of the food ingested. While it is true that marine fish swallow water as they breath, and so can obtain some benefit from vitamins in solution, I can see no added benefit over what is obtained when the vitamins are added directly to the food they eat. Therefore I view vitamins added to the water as pollution, but I'm sure many hobbyists would disagree with me, and that's ok. In no way do I intend to indicate that the nitrate "problem" is a result of the vitamins being in solution, however. Still, it might help the situation a little if you refrained from the practice of filling the water column with vitamins and just add a few drops to the food instead...this will make the vitamins last longer too...you are currently throwing away most of what you add as it is simply decomposing in the aquarium.

I emphasized "a little" a moment ago because this is what you need to do: take steps that each have a slight affect, and the combined effort will work a noticeable difference.

Now before I make some additional suggestions, I'd like to clear something up for you. While it is true that these fishes naturally live in water that has hardly a trace of nitrate, no-one has demonstrated any exact harm done to fishes by the nitrate which naturally accumulates in a closed system like yours as the endproduct of nitrification. In fact, if you were to call up some public aquariums that maintain large gravel bed filtered aquariums and ask them what their Nitrate readings were, you would be astounded. It is not unusual to find healthy fishes in systems running well in excess of 100 ppm nitrate. I have heard about readings approaching 300 ppm in a successful large aquarium containing many BIG fish and sea turtles...needless to say there was A LOT of food going into this tank... people just love to see divers hand-feeding the fish... I guess the beauty of the scene and the animals themselves isn't enough for most people.

So, what to do? Well, I see you have a protein skimmer. That's good. It has prevented your nitrate readings from going even higher. I am not familiar with the brand you mention, but I want to make clear that you cannot overskim a tank, so another skimmer or a larger or more efficient one will definitely have an impact on the amount of nitrate which accumulates. To avoid the witchcraft explanation, let me put it to you simply: The skimmer removes from the water the nitrogen rich amino acids which you add to the system as fish food. The more you skim out, the less nitrogen will be oxidized to

NO_3...nitrate. This is not necessarily the case when ozone is used in the skimmer. Use of a little ozone, say five to ten mg per hour, will usually "enhance" skimming by forming a stable foam, though the liquid collected may contain excess water...no real problem there. The use of a lot of ozone, however, actually prevents skimming by oxidizing the compounds that would have been skimmed off. This has some advantages, and may not be a disadvantage in some aquaria, ie. those which contain live rock, as I will shortly explain, but in your system or any sub-sand biologically filtered tank the result is enhanced nitrate formation. Provided the aquarium has a low fish population and is very lightly fed, the nitrate production in the presence of live rock is easily denitrified by facultative anaerobic bacteria within the rock, or absorbed and used by living plants on the rock and in living coral tissue. Yours is not a "reef tank" so I will not dwell on this further.

Nevertheless, you may borrow from "reefy" techniques to gain an advantage over your nitrate situation. You might consider increasing the light over your aquarium and introducing some *Caulerpa* algae. The best species for your situation are *Caulerpa mexicana* and *Caulerpa prolifera* as they are both fast growing and less prone than others to the sudden fruiting which usually results in loss of the plant. These plants will directly absorb NH_3, ammonia, which is freely liberated from your fishes' gills because you feed them. So, like the skimmer, the plants will remove nitrogen before it is converted to nitrate. These plants are capable of using nitrate as well, so they may directly lower the nitrate concentration. The only way to keep them working for you, keep in mind, is to prune them often...they remove the nitrogen from the water, and you must physically remove the plant growth from the aquarium to remove excess nitrogen. If you didn't, it would be akin to pouring the scum from your protein skimmer back into the tank.

Come to think of it, speaking of protein skimmers again, how did yours function when you added the vitamins? Typically they froth so much you have to shut them off to prevent loss of water onto the carpet. So you see, just adding the vitamins to the food instead of to the water will allow more continuous

operation of your skimmer as a reciprocal benefit.
Regarding water changes, ten gallons per month is fine,
but fifteen gallons per month might be better for your
particular set up. The gravel churning question is an
intriguing one because it brings up other interesting bits
of information. The algae which coat your gravel are
called cyanobacteria or "blue-green" algae despite the
fact that they occur in just about every color of the rainbow. They are nitrogen fixing, which means that they
take dissolved nitrogen gas, N_2, out of the water and
incorporate it in their tissue. In other words, these algae
are a source of nitrogen to your system beyond the food
that you add...the nitrogen which they incorporate is dissolved into the water from the atmosphere, but when
these algae die, they liberate amino acids back to the
water, and these are of course a potential source of
nitrate. So, technically yes, burying the algae contributes
to the nitrate level, but truthfully this is a very minor contribution compared with the fish food. Gravel stirring is a
good practice. If you wish to eliminate the growth of
cyanobacteria on the gravel, small herbivores such as
Turbo or *Astraea* snails and small hermit crabs will do
the trick. Their fecal pellets will be removed when you
siphon the gravel. Of course the plants and inverts I am
suggesting require that no copper treatments are made
in the aquarium.

I am certain that my recommendations here will give you
a handle on the problem. Some hobbyists employ denitrifying filters or nitrate removing media with varying
degrees of success. I am not recommending them to you
as I think you are better off attacking the problem at the
source rather than the end.*

*Jaubert's natural sys-
tem employing denitri-
fication in the gravel
substrate is an addi-
tional option here for
nitrate control. See
volume one of *Reef
Notes* and volume one
of *The Reef Aquarium*
for descriptions of this
technique.

Q. I have a question regarding protein skimming in
marine aquaria. I know that this topic is addressed regularly in your column, but I have not yet seen an answer
to this specific question. I have just recently added a
Sanders WT-250 protein skimmer to my Tenecor integrated system (filtration built in) 50 gallon reef tank.
I have read that protein skimming can remove trace elements from the aquarium water. Can protein skimming
also remove liquid vitamins, and macroalgae supplements?

Initially I was running the skimmer constantly, but have become worried that I may be depleting trace elements. Recently I have switched to running the skimmer on weekends, and shutting it off on Monday and adding the liquid supplements, and allowing the tank to run without the skimmer for four days. What do you think of this plan?

My other question regards lighting for Reef systems. (This issue being a tempest in a teapot --or aquarium--if there ever was one!) My lighting consists of two 24" tubes, one Triton 20 watt and one Philips 40 watt Actinic 03. I am not currently keeping any hard or soft corals, but would like to in the future. Do you think that this lighting is sufficient? (My anemones seem to be doing fine, but don't seem to be growing.) If I do increase the lighting, would you recommend doubling the number of fluorescent tubes, or do you feel Metal Halide is essential for keeping corals?
Sincerely, William S. Hildreth, Hollywood, Ca.

A. Well, since you asked, I don't like your plan. You said you have become worried. This worries me. Please refer to the previous answer...one's satisfaction with the aquarium should not be based on theory, but on the health and appearance of the aquarium instead. Let me go out on a limb here a moment and take a guess about the real reason you decided to change the operation of your skimmer. As I indicated in the previous answer, vitamins make the skimmer froth like crazy, causing the loss of too much water. I suspect that this occurrence in your aquarium, and the obvious need to shut the skimmer off when this happened, resulted in the rationalization that it was the thing to do. You put two and two together...the supplements made the skimmer froth too much, therefore it must be removing them, therefore it was doing an undesirable thing, right? Wrong...at least in my opinion. The skimmer should be operating continuously if you wish to maintain the highest water quality. You will have to refrain from adding too much stuff to the water. Fish obtain necessary vitamins and trace elements from the food. Inverts extract them from the water, but they are not harmed by the loss of some elements to the protein skimmer...think of your skimmer as just one more piece of coral or anemone...you wouldn't plan to remove your anemone for a couple of days each week for the hypothetical benefit of the other aquarium inhabitants. Water changes, fish feces and metabolites, and the addition of certain trace elements will meet the inverts' needs. If you do plan to keep hard corals, you will find that excess food additions are counter to the nutrient poor environment which they require...Less is more, get the picture?*

To continue with my amazing powers of intuition, I'll bet my best anemone that you're using the wrong ballast with that two-foot H.O 40 watt actinic. Pardon me for repeating the info again, folks, but a two-foot 40 watt H.O. bulb requires an 800 milliamp H.O. ballast to operate it at the proper color temperature...there are no exceptions here. Other ballasts such as a standard 40 watt, or electronic ones, may make the bulb light up, but do not fire it up to proper intensity.** The fact that you have only one H.O. tube made me suspect the wrong ballast...most people would not buy a $35 -$40 dollar ballast for just one little bulb. My apologies if I am mistaken.

Are you trying to bring the kettle to a boil again? No, you don't have to use metal halide lights to grow corals, but you may wish to use them...please review the photos and descriptions in the past two columns. Hobbyists will always be divided over the light sources they prefer, and that is fine as long as everyone is happy with their own results, theory and opinion be damned. Hobbyists looking to purchase a lighting system should base their decision on results seen in photos or in person, not on results heard or claims made. I don't know the dimensions of your 50 gallon tank, but if it is 48 inches long, then you would best scrap the two foot fixtures for the better option of using four-foot bulbs. Some very nice options for a four foot tank with four-foot bulbs are:

(2) H.O. 60W Actinic & (2) standard output 40W Daylight.
(2) H.O. 60W Actinic and (2) H.O. 60W Daylight.
(2) H.O. 60W Actinic and (4) 40W Daylight
(3) H.O. 60W Actinic and (3) H.O. 60W Daylight.
These four foot H.O. tubes use the same ballast as the

*Actually, when a very efficient protein skimmer is used, the addition of food benefits the corals. This mimics the situation on a reef: the water is nutrient poor but the corals provide shelter to fish that consume plankton and deposit their feces and ammonia in the vicinity of the coral. The presence of the fish enhances the corals' growth in the nutrient poor environment. Likewise food additions can stimulate coral growth when pollution is kept in check by protein skimming.

**My comments may not apply to newer electronic ballasts.

VHO 4' tube requires 1500 ma

two foot H.O. tubes, by the way. You may wish to try V.H.O. 110 watt tubes. These require a V.H.O. 1500 milliamp ballast.

If this 50 gallon aquarium is less than four feet long, then I recommend that you use at least three H.O. two foot Actinics and three H.O. two foot Daylight tubes. This would mean three double H.O. ballasts. If you wish to use metal halide, a single 175 watt 5500 kelvin degree bulb in combination with two Actinics (either H.O. or standard), or in combination with one Philips Actinic and one Philips Special Blue, would work well, but watch your temperature, and be careful about placing the fixture or stony corals too near to the water surface...let your experience be your guide. Hey, you might even consider a fixture using an Osram 250 watt powerstar... these are nearly 10 times brighter than the other combinations.*

*Other options include a minimum of 4 but ideally 6 standard fluorescent tubes with a good reflector. I don't exactly agree with my comments here regarding the number of metal halides. I recommend one metal halide per two feet of tank length for tanks less than 30 inches wide. So, if the tank is more than two feet long I should have recommended two metal halides instead of just one.

Q. Julian, My name is Jeff Joos. You published the picture of my elegance coral in your column a few months back. I wanted to write and keep you up to date on this coral.

The dots in my elegance coral did appear this year on June 30th. I saw them quite frequently after that, almost every day in fact. I haven't seen them for a couple of weeks now. I have to wonder if the elevated water temperature of the tank during the summer months isn't an important factor. I don't have a good thermometer but I would guess the temperature runs in the 82 - 83 degree range. The cooler temperatures outside have enabled my tank temp to run in the 76 to 78 degree range, and it has seemed to coincide with the coral not producing the dots any longer.

I was never able to witness the actual release of any of the dots. On several occasions I watched a dot travel up a tentacle, into the pink tip and then fall back down, but still remain in the tentacle to do the process over again. I have had trouble with my elegance not fully expanding this summer. After buying a water distiller and changing my lighting, I finally noticed the flame angel I had in the tank was picking at the coral. Through all of this harassment and not being fully expanded, I still saw the dots, more frequently in the evening. This past week I did a complete tear-down and netted the little devil angel and within the few days after my elegance seems to be doing much better.

Thanks for all the interest in my coral. It makes me feel as if I'm creating a good home for my corals. Also, I want you to know your column is the best of any that I read. Keep up the excellent work! Sincerely, Jeff Joos, Kettering, OH.

A. Thank you Jeff, for the info and complements. It will be interesting to see if the dots reappear when the temperature rises again. I think you made a very good observation regarding the flame angel and the less-than-usual expansion of the coral. This is a common occurrence which baffles many hobbyists, sending them off on a buying spree, as you indicated, to fix the situation. Many pygmie angels are just fine in reef tanks, but the occasional specimen will torment the corals. Flame angels have a 50/50 record of being coral pickers, in my experience. The sweet-faced lemonpeel angel has a worse record, being most likely of all the pygmies to feast on coral. I have recently noticed a pair of Venustus angels in one of the reef tanks I maintain has developed a taste for elegance coral, while a pair of Multifasciatus angels in the same tank has the occasional urge to eat open-brain coral, *Trachyphyllia geofroyi*. Fortunately the fish don't concentrate on destroying the coral, but their occasional bites appear to make the coral wince and thus remain only partially expanded. The frustrating thing about fish is that one can never predict how they will behave. Anyway, keep me posted on the observations of your elegance coral, Jeff.

Well that about does it for another month. Till next time, check out some of these articles, OK?

References
Amiel A.J., Friedman G.M., Miller D.S. (1973) Distribution and nature of incorporation of trace elements in modern aragonitic corals. *Sedimentology* 20:47-64.

Cross T.S., Cross B.W. (1983). U, Sr and Mg in Holocene

and Pleistocene corals *A. palmata* and *M. annularis. J. Sediment Petrol* 53:587-594.

Livingston H.D., Thompson G., (1971). Trace element concentrations in some modern corals. *Limnol. and Oceanog.* 16:786-796.

Nilsen A.J., (1990). The Successful Coral Reef Aquarium. *FAMA* 13:11

Pingitore N.E. Jr., Rangel Y, Kwarteng A., (1989). Barium variation in *Acropora palmata* and *Montastrea annularis. Coral Reefs* 8:31-36.

Pingitore N.E. Jr., Eastman M.P. (1985). Barium partitioning during the transformation of corals from aragonite to calcite. *Chem. Geol.* 48:183-187.

Shen G.T., Boyle E.A. (1988) Determination of lead, cadmium and other trace metals in annually-banded corals, *Chem. Geol.* 67:47-62.

Sprung J., Delbeek C. (1990). New Trends in Reef Keeping *FAMA* 13:12 p.8.

Thiel A. (1988). *The Marine Fish And Invert Reef Aquarium*, Ardvaark Press. Bridgeport, Ct.

Weber J.N. (1973). Incorporation of strontium into reef coral skeletal carbonate. *Geochem Cosmuchim Acta* 37:2173-2190.

June 1991

Nice tanks huh? Read on and you'll find out how they do it. The questions come first.

Q. I have bought a bottle of calcium chloride powder from a chemical company but I couldn't get any information regarding the usage. Currently I have a 55 gallon reef tank. Please direct me to the procedure of dissolving it in the water, and how much solution to add to the tank. Thank You, Kuang Min Huang, Newtown, Pa.

And a similar question...

Q. Dear Mr. Sprung,
I have been reading with interest the latest series of articles about water hardness in reef tanks, and the addition

of Kalkwasser to the tank to raise the hardness. I have a question or two about what exactly we are trying to do. First I have a question about what we can put in our tank, and what we shouldn't. Calcium oxide, calcium hydroxide, and now calcium chloride... I feel like I need to have a degree in chemistry to sort all this out. I went and bought some calcium chloride from a lab supply store, and added a little solution to the tank. Then I started to think what happened to the chlorine molecule when the calcium is stripped off. Is this something to be concerned about? I want the calcium level up, but I don't want to hassle with pH problems and carbon dioxide reactors to counteract the calcium.

What got me and a friend of mine interested in adding calcium was when we started putting calcium tablets from a health food store in our tanks. His was from oyster shell, mine was calcium carbonate. Is this the same as using the calcium products mentioned in the magazine articles? If the calcium tablets (calcium carbonate) will do the trick, then why mess with all the other chemicals? Robert N. Holder, Edwards, Ca.

A.Why mess with all the other chemicals? ...Because calcium tablets don't do the trick. I thought that this subject was well covered by Alf Jacob Nilsen's series and the article that Charles Delbeek and I put together, but it seems that there are still a lot of confused fish keepers out there, perhaps more now than ever because of the more focused attention to the topic of calcium hardness. Ok I'm going to spoon-feed this info to you this time, but in an abbreviated and hopefully simple-to-comprehend form.

Corals, mollusks, crustaceans and certain marine plants extract calcium from the water to build their skeletons. For optimal health and growth they need to draw this calcium from a "pool" of at least 400 ppm (same as mg/liter) of calcium in the water. Natural seawater contains approximately 400 mg/l calcium, and in the vicinity of reefs the level is typically even higher, between 450 and 500 mg/l. With average 25% per month water changes, the typical closed-system reef aquarium maintains a slightly deficient 250 to 350 mg/L of calcium in

"When a deep substrate is used, particularly when the aquarium contains many fish or big fish that respire a lot of CO$_2$, the contribution of calcium and alkalinity from dissolution of the substrate can be significant. This process is employed in Jaubert's system, described in *The Reef Aquarium Vol. One* and the first volume of this *Reef Notes* Series. Still, the dissolution of calcium carbonate gravel or sand usually does not meet the demand for calcium in a reef aquarium densely populated by rapidly growing stony corals. The addition of kalkwasser or other calcium supplements makes up for the difference. Kalkwasser has an advantage in that it precipitates phosphate in the aquarium, while the dissolution of natural calcium carbonate gravels can liberate some phosphate.

the water, depending on the density of calcium extracting organisms, frequency of water changes and the initial level of calcium in the salt mix used, and the amount of calcium in the freshwater added to make up for evaporation. This level of dissolved calcium can be expected whether calcite, crushed coral, oyster shell, and other buffering media are present or not... in other words they don't contribute significantly to the level of dissolved calcium in the water.* Our goal is to keep the level at or above 400 mg/L. Bear in mind that successful reef aquaria have, and can be maintained for years at deficient calcium levels; the purpose of maintaining elevated, more natural levels is to encourage real growth of stony corals and the proliferation of coralline algae, the latter benefit having the reciprocal effect of impeding the growth of filamentous algae.

Assuming we are starting with an established reef tank with the typical deficient calcium level of around 350 mg/L, we may quickly and safely elevate this level by either of two methods:

Method #1 Water change.

Method #2 Add a certain quantity of Calcium chloride
We CANNOT quickly elevate the level to 400mg/L using calcium hydroxide, "Kalkwasser", as I will shortly explain.

Important Note
I am not suggesting that any solution is best... there is no argument or difference of opinion involved... please read CAREFULLY... I am telling you when and how to use them.

Method #1 : Performing a water change replaces calcium deficient water with water at or above 400 mg/L of calcium. Several water changes or one big one could be employed to raise the level of calcium in the aquarium to the proper level. Of course this may not be practical or cost-efficient in the long run, but it is perfectly acceptable for the "quick-fix" needed to get the level up. Actually there is a new product which may make the maintenance of the calcium level by this method downright practical, if I may contradict my previous statement. While it is generally not my policy to specifically name brands, there is only one company so far that has foreseen the needs of reef-keeping hobbyists with respect to calcium in the artificial seawater mix, and that is Aquarium Systems, manufacturer of "Instant Ocean", with their new "Reef Crystals" salt. I mixed up a batch of this new salt and compared it to real sea water I collected in the vicinity of coral reefs. At the identical temperature and specific gravity, (full strength, approx. =1.026 s.g.), Reef Crystals measured approximately 524mg/L using the HACH test kit, nearly 100 mg/l more calcium than real sea water.

Method #2: The use of calcium chloride is very simple, and is by far the easiest way to elevate the level of dissolved calcium as high as you desire. Calcium chloride is very soluble in water. In other words, you can put a lot of calcium into a small amount of water. Compare this with calcium hydroxide which is not very soluble in water (at only about a gram and a half per liter). If you hold this very simple concept in your brain for just a minute*, it should be very clear to you why you cannot quickly raise the calcium level with $Ca(OH)_2$. You would have to add A LOT of water! Furthermore, calcium chloride does not significantly alter pH of the water, whereas "Kalkwasser" , the saturated solution of $Ca(OH)_2$, is very caustic with a pH of about 12. Calcium chloride is perfectly safe to use for the "quick fix," ie. to simply raise the dissolved calcium to the desired level, and the excess chloride ion added is insignificant with respect to the amount present in the water from the major dissolved salt, sodium chloride. But, to use calcium chloride for the maintenance of the calcium level, ie. regular additions as compared to the occasional one-shot boost, may not be such a good idea, especially in smaller aquaria, because of the accumulation of chloride ions and the resulting potential for undesirable effects from an ionic imbalance in the water. This is only theoretical, mind you, no one has documented any harm done. Still, it should be clear that calcium chloride addition is not intended as a routine maintenance procedure, but as a "repair" instead. So how do we maintain the calcium level once we've got it where we want it? with kalkwasser of course!

*Yes I was little bit condescending there.

Before I describe the use of kalkwasser again, let me offer a few pointers about calcium chloride. One should calculate approximately how much calcium chloride to add. Take for example the very straightforward situation of a 100 gallon aquarium at 350 mg/l dissolved calcium. If one wishes to boost the level to 450 mg/L, one needs to add 100 mg/L of calcium to the aquarium. At approximately 4 liters per gallon, this 400 liter aquarium would need 400 x 100mg =40 grams of calcium. Now comes the slightly tricky part...How many grams of calcium chloride are needed to get 40 grams of calcium? To calculate this precisely we need to know two things: the atomic weights of calcium and chloride, and the amount of water present in the stuff since it is hygroscopic (absorbs water from the air). In practice I neglect the water, aren't you glad? The atomic weight of calcium is about 40, of chloride about 35, but the formula is $CaCl_2$, meaning there are two chloride atoms for every calcium atom. It should be clear in the above simple example that one needs 40g + 35g + 35g =110g of calcium chloride. Adding a little extra, say a total of 125g of calcium chloride, approximately makes up for the neglected water molecules. The calcium chloride crystals are best dissolved first in pure R.O. and/or deionized water, but may simply be added to the sump of the filter without causing any harm...$CaCl_2$ dissolves very quickly. Do not add undissolved crystals directly into the aquarium, however, as they could injure the plants or invertebrates they fall on. By the way, feel the bottom of the container you are dissolving the calcium chloride in...pretty hot huh?

Kalkwasser is prepared by "dissolving" approximately 1 and1/2 to 3 grams of $Ca(OH)_2$ per liter in pure R.O. and/or deionized water. Adding the solution as make-up water to replace evaporation will maintain the proper level of dissolved calcium in the aquarium. Nilsen described the methods I am telling you about in detail in his series of articles just a few months ago, so please read them again, especially the article on calcareous water in the November 1990 issue of FAMA. It is important to add the kalkwasser slowly to avoid a harmful sudden rise in pH. The use of a dosing pump or drip system is preferred. Also note Nilsen's description of "high-quality" calcareous water, and his use of a simple reactor to provide it continuously...what he means is that fresh kalkwasser is much better than old kalkwasser, because the calcium falls out of solution with time. Those hobbyists who have CO_2 systems in operation on their aquariums are at an advantage here...they may add kalkwasser in large quantities without fear of the effect on the pH. The rest of us have to rely on the CO_2 produced by the aquarium's inhabitants to counter the rise in pH. Where there is a good fish and invertebrate population plus low levels of evaporation (and therefore small kalkwasser additions), CO_2 injection is not needed at all. High levels of evaporation necessitate the choice of one of two alternatives: Add the kalkwasser by a drip system at night when the lights are off and CO_2 production is high; or use only dilute kalkwasser solutions. Proceed slowly and watch the pH daily to determine the best procedure for your aquarium. Daily additions of kalkwasser are sufficient to maintain the level of dissolved calcium, and in time may slowly raise the level to about 500 mg/L depending on the depletion by the plants and invertebrates. It was my initial understanding that kalkwasser could only elevate the level to 400 mg/L, and maintain it there at a saturation point, but experience has now shown otherwise. Of course the Kalkwasser may not need to be added daily, or at full strength in order to maintain calcium levels above 400 mg/L. Nevertheless, Nilsen, Wilkens, Stüber, and other European hobbyists who have excellent success growing stony corals and coralline algae all agree that adding kalkwasser as make-up water is the way to do it.

*Calcium testkits are now available from various aquarium industry manufacturers, including Aquarium Systems, SeaChem, Red Sea Fish pHarm, Lamotte, and others.

Finally, you should have your own calcium test kit as a prerequisite to all of this madness. You may order your kit from HACH by calling 1-800-525-5940. Catalog number 1457-01, Model number HA-4R-MG-L.*

Some important bits of info they don't tell you, not directly at least:

**This applied to the HACH kit.

1- multiply the number of drops used in the titration by 8, (derived from the multiplication of the conversions given, 20 and 0.4), to get the level of dissolved calcium.**

2- The test measures accurately up to 400 mg/L, so to measure quantities above 400 mg/l, dilute the sample to 1/2 strength with pure water, using the sample measuring vial and the test vial to obtain one sample-vial-volume at 1/2 strength. Of course multiply the result by 2 (ie. the number of drops x 16 instead of 8.).

3- After several tests there is a noticeable buildup of calcium on the inside of the test vial. To maintain the level of accuracy, you should periodically fill the vial with vinegar for 30 minutes to dissolve off this calcium, and then thoroughly rinse and dry the bottle before running another test.

4- The reagents are very temperature sensitive! Do not leave the kit in your car! It must be maintained at room temperature at all times. It is a good idea to have a bottle of water of a known calcium level to use as a reference solution to check the quality of the reagents before each real test.

So there you have it, again. Now, it's time to find out about these tanks. The first Aquarium belongs to Mick Francis

Dear Julian,
Enclosed are a few photos of my 70 gallon reef tank. It has been set up for over 18 months now and as can be seen is doing well. The aquarium is lit by 4 fluorescent tubes with three more in the process of being integrated into the hood. At the moment I have 2- 40w Tritons and 2 -40w Philips Actinic 03's. Photoperiods are 2 tubes (one Actinic, one Triton) on for 12 hours and the other 2 tubes on for 10 hours. These lights are controlled by timers, the length of the time the lights are on varies from summer to winter. The tank also receives 1/2 to 3/4 of an hour of natural sunlight every morning.

The only equipment to be used other than the wet/dry filter is a Sanders WT250 protein skimmer, which is run on a continuous basis. A power head has also been added for more water movement to supplement the the Eheim hobby pump which runs the system.

I feed the corals occasionally, once every 2 to 3 months, with a mixture of Invert food and Artemia shelless brine shrimp eggs. I do not add any trace elements or supplements unless I can't do a water change. These water changes are carried out weekly (5 gallons) and also at the end of each month (10 gallons).

Temperature is maintained at 75 degrees F, although this temp. fluctuates from summer to winter, reaching 84 degrees F in Summer. Specific gravity is kept between 1.023 and 1.024, Nitrate is maintained at about 5ppm, Redox potential has never been measured.

All coral has been in the tank for 12 to 18 months, except for 1 or 2 bits of soft coral which have only been added in the last few months. Film used: Fuji 1600 ASA. Sincerely, Mick Francis, Sydney, Australia

Aquarium number two belongs to Fred T. Hutter

Enclosed I have 5 pictures of my 50 gallon mini reef, also the filtering system that came with the tank The filtering system was inside the tank in one corner. The fish I have in this tank are: 1 Flame Angel, 1 Six Line Wrasse, 1 Cardinal, 1 Chinese Goby, and 1 Watchman Goby. In addition to the corals you see in the pictures, I also have a brittlestar that is over 4 years old. The Flame Angel and Watchman Goby are over 3 years old. The Six Line Wrasse is 2 years 2 months old, the Cardinal is 1 year

Aquarium number two
belongs to Fred T. Hutter

*If Mr. Hutter was
referring to the
branchy soft coral on
the left side of the
photo, it is a *Sinularia*
sp., not *Capnella*.

and the Chinese Goby is 8 months old. The large leather
coral in the middle of my tank is four years eight months
old. When I purchased this specimen it was 4 inches
high and 2 inches wide. Now it is 13 inches high and 6
inches wide. (ed. note: at the base). All other corals are
over 1 and 1/2 years old. The bubble coral is three years
old. In one of the photos is something that I believe is
related to leather coral but I am not sure. Can you tell
me what it is? (ed. note: Of course...It is a *Capnella* sp.)*
Between the large leather coral and what I call a tree is
brown leaf type algae. I do not know the name of this.
(ed. note once again: I do. It is *Halymenia maculata*,
actually a red alga with rich brown, orange, and sometimes silvery pigmentation. It is a bit slippery to the
touch.).

On December 16, 1990 the readings were: S.G. 1.024, pH
8.1, Nitrate 0, dissolved oxygen 7.

I have modified the filter. In the last section of the filter
is the powerhead that pumped the water back into the
tank. I removed the powerhead and the DLS underneath
the head. I purchased a Mandarin I wet/dry filter. I put
the overflow where the (old) powerhead was. This was
installed 4/8/90. (I have replaced the spray bar with a
drip tray made for the filter, and I put bio balls in the dry
section and took out the DLS.)

The length of my tank, not including the part where the

filter is, is 38 inches. My lighting consists of :
4 - 18 inch Actinic 03 30 watt, and 4 - 36 inch Ultralume
50 30 watt. Two sets of two Actinics each are aligned
end to end to cover the tank length at the front and rear
(second to last) of the tank The Actinic 03's are powered
by the correct ballast as you mentioned in your column.

I have not fed any of my corals with any kind of food. I
feed my fish once every morning very sparingly so I
don't think that I'm overfeeding them. Sincerely, Fred T.
Hutter, Blue Bell, Pa.

Well, that does it for another Reef Notes. Oh, boy! wait
'till next month...

July 1991

Q. Dear Julian,
I have a 90 gallon reef set-up about 1 1/2 years old, I use
a trickle filter with DLS and inject air into the dry section.
There is nothing in the sump but a sponge filter, Also I
use a canister filter filled with three units of Chemi-Pure
and 20 oz. of research grade carbon, that discharges
behind the loose live rock wall (about 100 lbs) . My
lighting is 3 color tone 75's , 1 Triton bulb and 2 Actinics
(all are 40 w). They are on for 12 hours. Also I use powerheads in the tank and a protein skimmer full time. The
tank is stocked with:

1-green carpet anemone
1-elephant ear anemone
1-frogspawn coral
1-7" diameter plate coral
a colony of actinodiscus species
1 open brain coral
2 large xmas tree worms
1 small clam
2 firefish
1 mandarin goby
1 red lip blenny
2 coral banded shrimp
10 Turbo snails

Overall I would say everything looks great, the live rock
is blooming for lack of a better word. I have no algae

problems. The s.g. is 1.022, temp 76-79 degrees, pH 8.1, nitrate 1.2, KH 3.75 meq/L. I keep records so carbon and Chemi-Pure® are changed every 30 - 40 days. Water changes are 5 gals every 6 days using "reef" salt, I usually feed the fish every other day, but don't feed the inverts except about once a week I use live baby brine shrimp poured into the tank. My problem is that the frogspawn coral and the actinodiscus colony and to a lesser degree the anemones seem to cycle between shrunk up and fully open every day. They don't always do it at the same time ... is this normal? In all of the books I've read, I can't find what is normal behavior for inverts. I have not had any losses. Also my plate coral started turning dark about three days after I put it in, but it looks good. Is this to be expected? Tom Williams, Springfield, Mo.

A. Well Tom, although you've told me a lot, you were a little vague in the description of the problem, so it is difficult for me to tell exactly what is causing what you are observing. However, this gives me the opportunity to briefly go over the different stimuli for expansion and contraction in photosynthetic cnidarians, and maybe you can discover in my overview the cause or causes for what you are seeing. What you should see every day, Tom, is that your anemones and corals are "small" or contracted in the morning before the lights come on, and that they gradually "pump up" to peak expansion during the day, with maximum expansion tending to occur about 6 to 8 hours after the lights come on. After about 8 hours they begin to shrink up again, and within a few minutes after the lights go off, most are completely transformed. This cycle of expansion and contraction is a function of the cnidarians metabolism, and this is affected by 1- the photosynthetic rate, which is affected by the light intensity, and 2- the temperature, and 3- the amount of food ingested, both as solid particles and as dissolved inorganic nutrients. Food availability in the water may cause the sudden contraction or expansion of certain corals or anemones. Different species respond in different ways to a variety of amino acids contained in the food. When a photosynthetic cnidarian ingests food, be it solid or dissolved, the increase in its metabolism tends to make it expand in size, though too much food will cause prolonged contraction. A sudden temperature elevation may cause a brief expansion period, as the cnidarian attempts to increase its surface area to allow maximum diffusion in of the less soluble oxygen, but in the long run, high temperatures typically result in contraction or poor expansion of the coral or anemone, as it requires a certain temperature range in order to maintain its symbiosis with the zooxanthellae....more on this in a moment. Metabolism as controlled by the photosynthetic rate is a complex subject. A simple explanation might be that when a coral or anemone has received enough light = enough food produced by photosynthesis, it closes business for the day and shrinks up. Actually there may be some truth to this, but typically the coral or anemone is responding to a more pressing biological constraint. For instance, the process of photosynthesis by the zooxanthellae causes a build up of oxygen within the host's tissue.* You might wonder what's wrong with that, after all, corals and anemones need oxygen. Well, too much of a good thing ain't so good... in fact, in the case of oxygen, too much is downright toxic to them. (Lesser and Shick, 1989). Another result of illumination with high intensity light is that the tissues absorb infra-red light and may actually heat up, even when the water temperature is constant. As I indicated before, high temperatures are harmful, and usually produce contraction. I hope I have given you enough to work with. This entire subject will be covered in greater detail in a much awaited article Santiago Gutierrez and I have prepared.

*I covered this subject in *Reef Notes* volume one. Actually, it is the form of oxygen produced that is most harmful. High rates of photosynthesis, particularly stimulated by ultraviolet wavelengths, produce so-called active oxygen species such as peroxide and superoxide.

There is another range of causes for expansion and contraction, though not every cause will produce the cyclical nature you observed. Harassment by fishes will cause cnidaria to contract, as will aggression between different species of corals and anemones...sometimes even when no direct contact is made. Changes in the redox potential of the water, which may stem from a variety of factors, also do affect the appearance of the inverts. Elegance coral, for instance, expands during the day typically in direct proportion to the redox potential, and responds to changing trends in proportion to the change...expands as the redox rises and contracts as it falls. Leather corals, *Sarcophyton* sp., are very sensitive both to pH and redox potential, and they will respond to sudden changes in either by withdrawing their polyps and shrinking down. If they are really bothered by the change, leather corals will secrete a clear waxy film and stay closed for several days, until the film is shed off. Now you can look at your tank and figure which of these circumstances apply. Oh, about the plate coral, it has simply adjusted to the lighting in your tank by an increase in pigmentation...generally this indicates adaptation to a lower light environment than it was used to, and that is fine. Plate corals should be kept on the bottom of the tank, rather than on the rocks, because they normally occur on sand or coral rubble, and they have a habit of walking, which would send them tumbling down from the ideal perch if you chose to put them up on the reef.

Q. Dear Sir:
I am having major problems with my 55 gallon reef tank. I'll do my best to make a long story short... As I said, I have a 55 gallon tank with a wet/dry filter system. I use DLS for the dry filter, and crushed coral for the wet portion. I also have an in-sump protein skimmer. Hoping to avoid the expense of buying large quantities of live rock, I built a rock wall from rocks gathered from my front yard (I live in Florida and the rock is mostly fossilized sea bed). I then cycled the system with damsel fishes.

Once cycled I bought 4 or 5 small pieces of live rock. The rock contained a small colony of star polyps, a mushroom polyp, a small colony of button polyps and Florida false coral. Also in the tank are 2 clown fish and a mandarin goby, along with a feather duster worm. All this was added over the course of 4 to 6 weeks. I constantly monitor the water conditions, and there are no rises in ammonia or nitrite, nitrate or phosphates. Salinity and pH are stable.

Everything was fine up to this point, but then the problems began. The button polyps died within two weeks, but everything else was still doing great. I started getting a lot of micro-algae, so I bought 6 *Turbo* snails. Within hours they were all lying on the bottom of the tank! That's when I started getting worried - NOTHING kills snails!

Over the next few months I added a couple more pieces of live rock with no success. I also tried *Condylactis* anemones, but they all died within hours. I also added a few more snails, they all died. In fact, at this point everything has died with the exception of the fish, the feather duster, and a couple of other small tube worms on the live rock. They're all doing great!

I'm at the end of my rope, and everyone I have talked to about this problem is stumped. I tried partial water changes thinking it was something in my well water. I have changed at least 75% with bottled water, but the situation is no better. The tank has been up and running for 6 months, and the water conditions are: pH 8.3, S.G. 1.022, ammonia less than .25 ppm, Nitrite 0 ppm, phosphate less than 1 ppm, Temp 76 - 78 degrees. Any suggestions or advice would be greatly appreciated. Respectfully, Doug Sweet, Naples, Fl.

A. It is obvious from your description that some form of toxin is at work here. My best guess is that at some time a significant amount of pesticide was applied on your property, and the rocks from your yard absorbed it. It is not unusual for toxins to be selective in their effect on different forms of life. Now, would it not have been cheaper and would it not have caused less heartache to have started out with all live rock? My suggestion for you is to remove all of the Naples sea bed rock and return them to your yard where they may kill land snails and lizards for eons, which in turn would fertilize the ground around them and grow more plants, which would attract more snails and then...hey I think you could develop a new form of symbiosis between a living and a non-living thing! But seriously, you should make your reef out of living substrates, as this affords the most biologically stable environment. If your yard rocks were not poisoned, I bet you would have written me anyway, but about hair algae problems instead. Hair algae love to grow on bare limestone, but are repelled by coralline algae encrustations on live rock. If you plan to put more live rock in the tank, you must use seeded rock, or hold the new rocks in a separate aquarium with strong water movement for three to four weeks until they are seeded...You don't want to put new fouling rock into an established aquarium. If money is tight, just by a few choice seeded pieces of live rock at a time...you'll get there. I suggest that you remove the gravel from the wet portion of your filter...please read my often repeated comments about this in previous columns. Also, I wonder how much gravel you have on the bottom of your tank...it should not be more than 1/2 inch for now, unless you have many pistol shrimps, sea cucumbers, sleeper and watch-man gobies to sift through it all the time. Best of luck with the new beginning.*

*It is possible that a dinoflagellate bloom was killing the snails and that other affected creatures died from unrelated causes. This would have meant that the rocks were not the cause. It is impossible to know for sure what was happening here without seeing the tank. I'm reasonably confident that my advice was correct. For additional information about toxic dinoflagel-late blooms please see volume one of this series and *The Reef Aquarium*, Vol. one.

I'd like to take a moment to inform you again about the status of live rock collecting in Florida, as I haven't done so for over a year, and a change has occurred which affects everyone who keeps reef tanks. If you have been following this saga, and believe me you should, the cur-rent situation allows the harvest of live rock in Federal waters but not in state waters. This legislation was intended to protect reefs and rocky shore areas within state waters, but had the unforeseen side effect of redi-recting and concentrating rock collection on to the Florida Keys reef tract, since this area has shallow, prime rock collection zones beyond the three mile limit that defines state waters on the Atlantic coast. Well, now it seems the intention in the long run is for the complete end to live rock collection in Florida, and the gradual phase-in of aquaculture. The state's planned way around the federal waters loophole is to make it illegal to bring live rock to shore in Florida. At a hearing called in Tallahassee I spoke to Georgia Cranmore, an Ecologist who wrote "Policy Options Regarding Live Rock" which she presented to the Marine Fisheries Commission. I indicated to her, as I did in front of the commissioners, that I thought aquaculture was a good idea, and that it would be nice as another rock option for hobbyists, but I thought the live rock harvest should be allowed to con-tinue. When I asked her about competition with Florida "farmed rock", from natural sources in cheaper foreign markets she quickly answered, "Don't worry about that."

Actually, I wasn't really worried until I pressed further and asked what she really meant. "There won't be any

At this point the live rock issue is almost a dead issue. It is 1996 and harvest of wild live rock will cease shortly. One encouraging development is that the state of Florida has made some efforts to simplify the permitting process for bottom leased aquaculture and there are several companies already growing live rock on their lease sites. It will even be permissible to harvest such aquacultured rock if it has live stony corals on it. There are also several inland coral farms growing corals and live rock.

Shipments of live rock from the Indo Pacific have continued, and hopefully will continue.

competition," she said.

Now that's a scary thought! Could she know something we don't about the fate of the marine aquarium hobby? I tend to think she did not appreciate the full scope of this assertion, and that she was merely expressing her own view and wish...but who knows?

I'll tell you what, hobbyists and retailers, it is to your great advantage to take a moment now, before the decisions are made, and let her know how the ban of all live rock (Hawaii and Florida may be just the beginning, folks) affects you, both from an economic and educational standpoint. No hate mail please, I trust you will sincerely demonstrate the broad impact this type of legislation has.

Please write to: Georgia Cranmore, ecologist, and Russ Nelson, executive director State of Florida Marine Fisheries Commission, 2540 Executive Center Circle West Suite 106, Tallahassee, Fl. 32301. Hey, you can fax them, if you prefer: Fax # 904-487-4847. Don't delay!

Next month I promise to show you a very unusual reef tank that Bruce Carlson has behind the scenes at the Waikiki Aquarium, with exquisite and fast-growing stony corals he has collected in Fiji and Palau.

References
Lesser, M.P., and Shick, J.M. (1989). Effects of irradiance and ultraviolet radiation on photoadaptation in the zooxanthellae of *Aiptasia pallida*: primary production, photoinhibition, and enzymic defenses against oxygen toxicity. *Mar. Biol.* 102: 243 - 255

August 1991

As I promised, we begin this month with a view behind the scenes at the Waikiki Aquarium. Take it away Bruce.

February 17, 1991

Dear Julian,
Thought You might enjoy seeing our outdoor experimental coral tank once more. The growth of the corals in this tank has been extensive. You may recall the purple-

brown *Montipora digitata* from Palau which was only a bunch of broken branches last year. As you can see from photo #1, the colony is now 20" x 6" x 5" tall. The only thing stopping it is where it comes in contact with other corals (the *Montipora* usually loses). More interesting to me are the *Acropora* corals. I collected twelve colonies in Fiji last June and you can see some of them in the two photos. Three of them have doubled in size since June, and as you can see they are retaining their colors beautifully! The corals which are visible in the photos include:

Photo #1 (left to right)
Caulastrea furcata (Fiji)
Lobophyllia sp. (Palau)
Pavona cactus (out of focus w/white rim, Palau)
Montipora digitata (foreground, Palau)
Acropora spp. (Fiji)
Tridacna maxima

Photo #2
mostly *Acropora* spp.
Seriatopora hystrix (out of focus, foreground, Fiji)
Platygyra pinni (Palau)
Goniastrea? sp. (Fiji)
Lobophyllia sp. (Palau)
two unidentified Faviid corals
Tridacna maxima (same specimen as above)
This tank also contains:
Stylophora pistillata (two, Fiji)
Pectinia lactuca (Palau)
Heliofungia actiniformis (three, Palau)
Euphyllia ancora (Palau)
Plerogyra sinuosa (three, Palau)
Moseleya latistellata (Palau)
Tridacna gigas (one, Palau)
T. derasa (eight, Palau), *T. crocea* (25, Australia)

You may recall that when you visited here last year, many of the corals had recently died back after the tank accidentally drained. The *Pavona cactus* that you saw "dead", has re-grown from the four tiny slivers that I found on the bottom of the tank after the catastrophe. Each of those slivers measured about 1/4" long last year;

Photo #1

I just measured the colony (all four pieces combined) a minute ago and it is now 2.5" in "diameter" and the branches average 2" high! You can barely see the white edging on the branches in the background of photo # 2- keep in mind that the photo was taken last November and it is larger today.

I don't know if you will want to mention this tank to your readers, but it is certainly unique. Photo #3 shows the tank's exterior appearance. It is a plastic tank about 4' on each side, the water depth is about 2', and it holds about 120 gallons of natural seawater. Circulation is provided by the 30 gallon surge tank mounted above and to one side of the tank, supplemented by the undergravel filter air-lift tubes. There is no additional filtration, but this tank is not a closed- system. We have access to seawater (filtered with no plankton) from a well, and a steady drip of water is added to the tank at a rate of about 2.5 gallons/hour (visible coming from the tap on the left side of photo #3). While I realize this is different from most home aquariums, I think it could be "upgraded" to a closed system and would still work. Outside, my main concerns are temperature and evaporation but the steady flow of replacement water seems to suffice.

The sun-and-surf-loving corals, such as the *Acropora* are located on the top of the rocks, while the corals requiring less intense light and less severe water motion, such as the bubble corals, are on the sides. Algae is controlled by one yellow tang, *Zebrasoma flavescens* ; one blue tang,

Photo #2

Paracanthurus hepatus, and two flame angels, *Centropyge loriculus,* and there is one wrasse, *Coris venusta,* in the tank. Lighting is strictly sunlight and there are no overhead filters to eliminate ultraviolet light. The tank has been cleaned once in the past four years (because it is outside, a lot of air-borne debris eventually accumulates inside). I do no maintenance on the tank, except to periodically care for the pump operating the surge tank, change the airstones, and other miscellaneous activities.

*Times have changed! Reef Aquarists are now growing and propagating many *Acropora* species and other small polyped stony corals, including offspring from Dr. Carlson's aquariums.

I doubt that very many coral-keepers anywhere are maintaining *Acropora** and other branching corals such as these. Obviously, they can be kept successfully in captivity and eventually I will try keeping them under completely artificial conditions indoors. We do have *Acropora* in our main coral exhibit which has been there for nine years, but it is not as vibrant in color nor has it grown as much. The sunlight in the tank passes through a plexiglass skylight so most of the UV light is filtered out -- the UV probably stimulates the production of the brightly colored pigments. Secondly, the indoor tank does not have the strong surge action which is provided in the outdoor tank. I'd recommend to aquarists if they want to keep *Acropora* , beef up the water motion, use a larger tank, and use sunlight or the best and brightest artificial light available. Many of the Pacific *Acropora* corals live in the surge zone and some are even completely out of water and exposed to sunlight (or torrential rain!) at low tide! In my opinion, this is the kind of coral reef tank that will give us all a real challenge to

Photo #3*

maintain in the future. It certainly looks more like a real south seas reef, as opposed to most mini-reefs which simulate lagoon environments!

I didn't want to write an article today, but I do want to mention the treatment of sick corals. Right on schedule this year, our ten year-old *Euphyllia ancora* in our indoor reef tank started to develop white areas as soon as winter arrived (the tank is shaded in the winter and receives dimmer metal halide lighting from a 400 watt bulb). The "apparent" cause, as before, were countless numbers of ciliate protozoans. I treated the coral in the usual way by dipping it for one minute in fresh water, as I mentioned to you when you were here. The colony now weighs at least ten pounds and is very large so this wasn't easy. It was maintained in an isolation tank and treated once more about a week later. After two weeks in quarantine, it fully recovered (except for the dead areas) and is now back on display. I have used this technique successfully on a number of different corals (including this specimen on numerous occasions), but bubble corals seem to be more sensitive to the freshwater treatment. If you want to pass this note on to your readers, go ahead, but caution them that the corals I am treating are otherwise in good condition, except for the areas being destroyed by protozoans (this condition is not unlike the white-band disease described in field situations, but it may turn out to be a different cause). This technique may be too stressful on corals recently obtained.

*Ed is now at the Tampa Aquarium.

One final point: all of the corals collected in Fiji last year were shipped home "dry". Ed Bronikowski, now working at the National Zoo*, presented a paper several years ago that this technique will work, and it does! I collected only small colonies (with permission from the Fiji government!), wrapped them up in strips of plastic to serve as a cushion, placed them in plastic containers just large enough to fit them, dunked them in seawater then drained all but a tablespoon out, placed the container inside a plastic bag filled with oxygen, then packed them as usual inside a styrofoam-lined box. With almost all the water removed, the box weighed very little. All of the corals survived the 15

hours between packing and unpacking.
Best regards,
Bruce A. Carlson, Director, Waikiki Aquarium

Thanks Bruce for taking up nearly half of my column! - and thanks for taking the time to share your experience. I wanted to add a few comments... Through Alf Nilsen and Charles Delbeek I have been made aware that there are hobbyists in Germany, Switzerland, Norway and elsewhere who practice the so-called "Berlin School" of thought in aquarium keeping...They maintain reef aquaria with live rock, protein skimming, high intensity lighting (usually Osram HQI TS/D 250 watt powerstars combined with blue fluorescents), and strong water motion (usually provided by several Turbelle pumps controlled by a pulsing device or "powertimer"), the daily addition of Kalkwasser as make-up water, and periodic additions of strontium chloride solution. No external biological filters are incorporated in the system. (please see New Trends In Reefkeeping Dec. 1990 FAMA) These hobbyists have been quietly growing *Acropora* and other stony corals for years. In fact, one of the first to succeed in this endeavor in a closed system, Mr Dietrich Stüber, has given away over one thousand branches of *Acropora* from a colony which began growing in his aquarium in the early 1980's.

*I was wrong about the identification. It is *Pocillopora damicornis*.

I have a beautiful colony of *Seriatopora** growing in my aquarium that has grown from a small branch given to me by Alf Nilsen, who broke it off of a large colony in his aquarium, which grew from a branch given to him by Dietrich Stüber. We really have come a long way in the art of reef aquarium keeping, though, as Bruce correctly points out, in North America we haven't really caught on with the interesting and fast growing stony corals found on the reefs. This is at least partly due to the fact that these corals have not been made available to us. We have seen a good supply for years of the lagoon species, ie. Elegance, Bubble, Hammer, etc., but whether due to lack of demand, or restricted entry by CITES, we have seen no *Acropora* sp.**

**As I said, times have changed. Now all sorts of stony corals are available from

I want to add one more detail to Bruce's recommenda-

Indonesia, Fiji, the Solomon Islands, and elsewhere. Furthermore, many of these species are also available now as tank raised fragments or whole colonies. We have come a long way in just a few years!

tions for the care of *Acropora* sp. I think that one of the most significant factors in the successful culture of *Acropora* in a closed system is the addition of strontium chloride. Before such additions in my own aquarium, *Acropora* species merely lasted about two months on average, sometimes holding out as long as four months before either the tissue just disappeared in a manner that also looked very much like white band disease, or the coral would suffer the attack of protozoans which left a trail of white skeleton behind a brown jelly-like front of attack. I am now growing six colonies (obtained from a permitted collector) in two aquaria, and frankly the only variable which separates my present success from previous failure is the addition of strontium. All of the colonies have grown markedly, an inch or more on each branch tip in only a few months, and many new branches have appeared. The polyps are always out, and there has been no incidence of tissue loss or infection.

As I explained a few months ago, strontium chloride solution is prepared by making a 10% stock. This stock solution is added at a rate of 2 milliliters per 25 gallons of aquarium per two weeks. I have one correction to make on my original recommendation in this column. Initially I suggested that it was preferable to add the solution daily, ie. divide the above figure by 14, but upon further experimentation and experience I can assure you that it is unnecessary to be so fussy, and that a full two weeks dose or even a slight overdose presents no problem...I have witnessed no toxicity related to strontium, though I would be cautious still about exceeding the recommended dosage which might result in accumulation in the long run.... which might be undesirable.

Q. Dear Julian,
I have kept fish for some 27 years with good success. Nothing fancy, just the basic freshwater stuff. Over the years I have had very little problems with excessive algae. That was until we moved recently, my water now comes from a private well. I noticed right away that there was a difference and believed it to be excess nutrients in the water. Recently I set up a 55 gallon marine fish tank (Fluval external filter with Siporax and under-

gravel filters with powerheads). Even before the tank was cycled, a slimy brown algae film covered everything. I talked to some people about this and they seemed to think that this is a normal phase and that it will go away as the more desirable green algae appear. I also read that this can be the result of poor lighting so I added some good fluorescent lamps and started over again. Again the slimy stuff appeared right away. Do I have a problem? Since I live in a rural area I am kind of on my own. It was with great interest that I read your response to a letter from Philip Lockie in your Reef Notes/FAMA March '91 in which you recommend the use of reverse osmosis. I asked several people about r.o. and was told that it would not make any difference as the nutrients will be added back to the tank and that the marine salt itself contains nutrients. Since the cost of an r.o. system is high I prefer not to rush out and buy one without additional info. Can you help me with any info and/or reading references? Thanks much, Bill McGinnis, Annandale, Mn.

A. For reading materials I suggest you go to your local public library where there should be plenty of info on water purification. Also the manufacturers of various r.o. units should be willing to give you info about what theirs are capable of doing. What you are witnessing is most likely diatom growth. Diatoms are a special type of algae which make glass skeletons of incredible design...to you their skeletons look like white powder when you see them in a diatomaceous earth filter, but under a microscope they are really something to look at. In aquaria, however, they are not so much of a sight for the eyes, as you have noticed. Fortunately their growth is severely limited when you limit the crucial building block of their skeletons, silicate. In my experience, r.o. sufficiently removes the silicate so that diatom growth is limited. I have read claims that r.o. is not very effective at removing silicate, and I have read just the opposite. I try not to give as much importance to what I read as to what I actually see and experience. You might also add a few snails and/or a *Ctenochaetus* sp. Tang to your tank, as they will graze on the diatoms, and their lightweight fecal pellets are easily trapped and removed via a mechanical filter. In this way they export the silicate which has been removed from the water by the diatoms. In time your aquarium will support very little diatom growth. However, if you add silicate just once with new water, whammo! overnight they will return...and they will subside again if you keep limiting their silicate source by using purified water. There is also information in marine botany literature about the use of germanium dioxide to impede the growth of diatoms. Germanium is very similar to silicate and the diatoms soak it up, but they are rendered unable to make their skeletons, so they stop growing. This practice is useful when natural seawater is being used in static open systems to culture specific plants or invertebrates, but it is unnecessary in closed system aquaria where diatom growth can be limited more directly. There are many water purification options out there, and they are not all that expensive, so I would shop around, read their literature, and consult hobbyists who can demonstrate (not just talk about) the efficacy of the unit they recommend. Good luck to you.

May your corals be a bloomin' and a growin'.

October 1991

Q. Dear Julian,
I finally got my film developed of an event that happened in my tank. My 120 gallon tank had been set up for a little under 2 years when I saw this occur. The urchins came in on my live rock when I first set up the tank. Their body width is about 2 inches wide.

The photos clearly show the urchins spawning. The date this happened was January 26 of this year, in the middle of the afternoon. I noticed the water being abnormally cloudy and looked to see the problem and discovered the urchins. They were perched on the highest rock point in my tank when this happened. I wanted to share this event with you and possibly the readers of this magazine which you write for.

Keep up the good work you are doing with your column. It is my favorite of the different hobby magazines that I read. Sincerely, Jeff Joos, Kettering, Oh.

You are only saying that because this is the third time your name has appeared in my column...you keep up the good work, Jeff, OK? Those look like *Arbacia punctulata* urchins, which means that your rock probably originated from the Gulf of Mexico. Thanks for the compliment and photos.

Q. Dear Julian,
While my question is not specifically reef related, it might still be of interest to your readers, and hopefully worthy of your comments. I've been unable to successfully maintain *Centropyge* angelfish and desperately need some advice on how to do so. Despite my best efforts to provide these fish with a stable aquatic environment and a wide variety of quality frozen and live foods (my understanding is that erosion is caused primarily by a nutritional deficiency), my dwarf angels begin exhibiting signs of head erosion in four or five months. The angels appear healthy in all other respects and the rest of the tank's inhabitants are thriving.

My inability to keep dwarf angels is particularly disheartening, since it was this genus that lured me to the marine side of the hobby after keeping freshwater fish quite successfully for years.

Any advice you have regarding prevention or reversal of erosion (lateral line disease) would be greatly appreciated. Sincerely, John Boghosian, Lindenhurst, IL

A. I'm sure I won't have to tell you to listen up folks, because it seems the mere mention of lateral line erosion commands everyone to a hushed attention. Let me start off by telling you a few things. It is not my intention here to give you a difinitive answer and, as you will soon understand, there is none. I also do not intend to discourage you either, for there is hope for your plight, as you should see in the variety of perspectives concerning this ailment which I will present. I know that I may generate more questions here than answers, but I hope that this is what is needed to inspire a serious attempt at understanding the many aspects of head and lateral line erosion. After all, this is the topic that got me started in this magazine (see FAMA Dec. 1982 Disease prevention and control, and April 1984 editorial).

The study of lateral line erosion presently consists of a little bit of science and a whole lot of speculation based on anecdotal observation. Furthermore, while we ascribe to one conceptual ailment the symptoms of pigment and tissue loss in the face and lateral line, it is clear that there are several distinct ailments which affect different fish, and even the same fish; likewise these have distinct causes. Blasiola (FAMA May 1990) covered that aspect quite well and offered some suggestions for dietary improvement, with particular emphasis on vitamin c. He also described a supposedly irreversible condition, a kind of tumor, which affects the nerves in the face of certain fish. Remember always that the symptoms of head and lateral line erosion in your fish could be the result of many different factors, and could actually be several different ailments, some of which I will briefly discuss now.

Pathogen(s)?
I am aware of at least three qualified pathologists who claim to have found an organism associated with the condition in certain fishes. This is most encouraging since it offers the possibility of a theraputic cure in some instances. Two of these people are apparently preparing papers on their findings, so we will soon have more practical advice on this subject. Personally, I am curious about the slowly progressing, smooth-edged form of fin

rot which often acompanies the head and lateral line erosion, especially since I have often (I did't say always folks) witnessed such erosion beginning on the fins before spreading to the face and lateral line. I feel that this suggests the involvement of an organism. On the subject of this smooth fin erosion, I had an eerie experience last year when I surveyed Carysfort reef after reading about massive loss of living corals there in a National Geographic article. As I was just beginning to recover from the shock of seeing acres of dead elkhorn coral (*Acropora palmata*), and the bizarre sight of newly dead snow-white branches with red and green slime algae on them...just as if they came out of an aquarium, I saw dozens of schooling adult blue tangs (*Acanthurus coeruleus*) with scalloped and eroded caudal, dorsal, and anal fins. I did not see any head or lateral line erosion on them, but I believe that the eroded fins were the same preliminary symptom as I have seen in aquaria. I wondered then if the unusually abundant growths of cyanobacteria (slime algae) on this reef had anything to do with the condition of the tangs, considering that slime algae are often covering dead decorations in the typical fish aquarium. Of course this presents a whole other possibility, so be it, I'm just telling you what I saw.

*I have not explored this site or notion any further but still wonder about the possibility of a connection between cyanobacteria and this condition. The appearance of these tangs in the natural environment was quite astonishing.

**A very interesting article by Indianapolis Zoo Curator Steve Collins in Aquarium Systems' SeaScope Summer 1995 issue describes the effect of supplementing the diet with foods rich in vitamin A. As with so many other successful cures of this condition, it worked very successfully! I don't mean to belittle the results. In fact they are compelling. I really suspect this approach may be especially helpful.

Diet

As you noted, John, diet often plays a role in the onset of this condition, and sometimes it may be the key factor which can be modified to effect a cure. Many of the fish most commonly afflicted with the condition are herbivorous, or have diets with substantial intake of plants...this may be not so obvious as in the case of, say, the butterflyfishes, which eat corals as a substantial part of their diet. As they consume the coral animal, so too do they consume the symbiotic Zooxanthellae algae. Many hobbyists have observed spontaneous cures of symptoms shortly after placing fish in an aquarium where there is a lot of algae to graze on, or shortly after the inclusion of more algae in the diet via frozen or fresh foods. Still, this does not work a miraculous cure every time, and not all afflicted fish are herbivores. which leaves the aquarist baffled and doubting the word of those who emphasize the dietary link to this problem. A dietary link for carnivorous fishes could include vitamin deficiency or a special requirement for cetain amino acids only contained in live foods. As another side note, I remember when I was visiting the Waikiki aquarium a little over a year ago, Marj Awai told me about a study done on Surgeonfishes, which naturally have certain organisms living within their gut that presumably assist them with digestion, or with the assimilation of important nutrients. The study showed they may lose these organisms once collected and placed in a captive environment. Apparently these organisms depend on the Tang's dietary range of numerous species of naturally occurring algae. I remember immediately thinking, Ahah!, lateral line disease, but as far as I know no one has linked the condition to the loss of specific gut fauna...another avenue for research.

Trace Elements
If dietary improvement alone can lead to spontaneous cure in some cases, a question arises concerning the exact property of the algae which effects a cure. Perhaps the algae provide a natural form of antibiotic which helps the fish fight an organism causing these symptoms, perhaps it is just vitamins, as suggested by Blasiola...or perhaps the algae contain one or more essential elements, or compounds that are otherwise lacking in the aquarium and fish's diet. I have wondered about iodine depletion via skimming and chemical filtration, and I have wondered if perhaps a specific organic form of iodine in the algae might also be important in the cure effected by the algae. In nature, algae concentrate a variety of trace elements and compounds which could be important to the herbivores' diet. Algae growing in our aquaria, however, may be deficient in certain respects, so that in some cases it might not provide the spontaneous cure that wild-caught algae can. Please bear in mind that this is hypothetical.*

*I experimented with iodine additions and found they had no affect on this condition.

Chemical irritants
This factor is difficult to prove, but many hobbyists, myself included, have observed rapid onset of head and lateral line erosion symptoms in certain fish associated with water treatments such as copper sulfate. Noxious chemicals, or merely foreign chemicals to the natural

marine environment have been implicated for years in conversations among aquarium hobbyists, as a significant factor in the occurrence of these symptoms. Many times I have heard the suggestion that even the typical accumulation of Nitrate in a closed system is a factor, but no controlled experiments have been performed to show this, as far as I know. Considering the range of suspected factors, truly controlled experiments are most difficult to perform.

Carbon

It would seem that the use of activated carbon would curb the occurrence of symptoms because of its ability to remove noxious chemicals from the water, and so indeed some hobbyists have linked activated carbon use, again, anecdotally, to spontaneous cure or improvement of symptoms. Still more hobbyists, however, have included the use of activated carbon on the list of the most certain causes of head and lateral line erosion symptoms.* It is a typical situation in the marine aquarium hobby to have two groups of aquarists saying (and sometimes even experiencing) precisely the opposite thing. So why might some or all activated carbons cause the onset of these symptoms? A study by Tom Frakes of Aquarium Systems may soon provide an answer. Tom has observed the onset of symptoms in the Domino damselfish brought on by the use of activated carbon, and is currently attempting a controlled study. Two possible factors come to mind, though this does not mean that they are the only possibilities. First, it is possible that the carbon itself leaches some noxious compound(s) into the water, and so it may be a chemical irritant. Second, the effect might be due to the carbon's removal of an essential trace element, even though fishes generally obtain what they need from their food....perhaps this works in conjunction with a dietary deficiency.

*I have witnessed this effect with some types of activated carbon but not with others. I feel confident that the effect is a result of some irritant coming off the carbon rather than something removed from the water by the carbon. It is possible that carbon dust produced by tumbling of the granules in strong water flow could be such an emitted irritant.

Sunlight?

I have heard from reliable sources that spontaneous cures of symptoms have been achieved by placing affected fish in (chilled) aquaria that receive a lot of direct natural sunlight. Granted the availability of algae to these fish is the most likely reason for the success, but two other possibilities exist which should be addressed.

One is that the light could help the fishes manufacture vitamin D as it does in people... I don't know if this works in fishes. The other is that the U.V. irradiation could eliminate a disease organism.

Electrical charge?

Now here's a new one for you folks. Very recently I got a call from Dick Boyd who related the experience of a hobbyist calling him about a most intriguing observation. The hobbyist, Dan Hensler, measured a significant electrical charge in his aquaria, and decided to ground them by attaching a grounded wire to a stainless steel hose clamp bent over the edge of the aquarium and in contact with the water. This change resulted in dramatic behavioral improvement in a formerly skittish tang, and initiated healing in two stubborn cases of lateral line erosion in a Passer's and a Flame Angelfish, the latter benefit being of particular interest to you, Mr. Boghosian. The aquaria in question already had grounded pumps and grounded light fixtures. Nevertheless, when either of these items was on, a charge could be measured in the aquarium, and the charge was different when the pump was on only, versus the lights only. Mr. Hensler's observation provides a serious question... could these electrical devices generate a charge in the water by induction? I ask you, is it possible that we professional aquarists have missed a very important consideration? No doubt we will see more about this. The link with head and lateral line erosion is most attractive since the cure in this instance is easy, and the cause seems plausible... the charge could irritate the heavily innervated lateral line.*

Certainly more can be said about head and lateral line erosion too, but I leave it up to you all to keep on trying and let me know of your successes and failures... good luck!

Q. Dear Julian,
I know you've covered this before, but I have a bristle-worm problem. I can't keep anemones for more than a few days because the worms destroy them.
The tank is a 55 gallon, half filled with live rock. I've removed the substrate as you suggested. It is filtered by

*After this discovery there was suddenly a demand for a new product called a grounding probe. The probes have a titanium tip and connect with the grounding screw on a wall outlet via a long wire. Reports on the effect of this device on lateral line disease have been mixed, are anecdotal and inconclusive. In my opinion grounding probes are not the miracle cure they have been called by some people, but they do work to eliminate induced charges. It is important to note that the probe should be located as close to the source of the charge as possible, as there can be an "invisible wire" effect wherein the charge traveling from its source to the probe could disturb fish crossing the path. If the source of the charge is the water pump in the sump, locate the probe in the sump. If it is a powerhead in the tank, locate the probe near it.

a wet dry, protein skimmer with ozone at 5 mg per hour. I don't feed the tank and the fish and corals are doing well (1 *Centropyge eibili*, 1 Scopas tang, 2 Yellowtail Damsels, 5 soft corals, 1 Hammerhead Coral, and several *Turbo* snails), and one leather coral has reproduced.

I tried baiting a nylon bag with shrimp and scallop as you suggested numerous times, but only once had any luck (when I couldn't sleep at 2:00 AM). Needless to say, I can't do that continually. By limiting the nutrients, I had hoped to starve them out, but they are thriving.

Is there some natural enemy to the worms, perhaps a shrimp or a crab, that would eat the worms and not bother the other inhabitants? I've tried a banded coral shrimp recently and it ignored them. Aside from the bristleworm problem, everything is doing very well, but I would like to keep anemones and be rid of the worms. Sincerely, Larry Clark, Vancouver, Wa.

A. Hey, if the worms destroy anemones in a few days, you might try baiting a nylon stocking with an anemone! I'm only half serious with that recommendation, Larry. I do have a couple more suggestions for you, but that's all. As for natural predators, I am aware of a couple more you might try, but cannot guarantee that they will be interested in your worms either. The adorable bird wrasse has a reputation for eating bristleworms, so you might want to give it a try. Likewise the arrow crab is also supposed to have a taste for them. Arrow crabs tend to grow large and threaten small fish, but otherwise they are pretty tame. If your rocks are tightly packed, Larry, even if you removed the substrate as I suggested, then there will always be a large refuge area for the worms where the predators can't get at them...a more open reef structure helps prevent this. Finally, I have noticed that a sudden drop in specific gravity (say, from 1.022 dropping to 1.018) will sometimes drive worms out into the open where they may be removed easily. I worry about making that kind of recommendation because while I know that I can safely drop the S.G. in an aquarium, I don't know if you have the experience to do it as safely...so be careful if you wish to try it!*

*It is essential to add buffer to the water to maintain alkalinity when you dilute the specific gravity.

Pseudochromis spp. such as *P. fridmani* and *P. springeri* are good worm eaters. Please refer to *The Reef Aquarium, Vol One* for additional info about bristle worms.

Well, I had planned to talk about iodine in more detail,

but I got a little carried away on the lateral line topic, so you will have to wait, ...so what else is new?

November 1991

This month we start on the subject of iodine.

Iodine may be used in the aquarium in several different forms. The most commonly used form is potassium iodide. The stock is prepared by adding 25 grams of potassium iodide to half a liter of pure water. This is added to the aquarium at a rate of 1/2 ml per twenty-five gallons per two weeks. Other options for sources of iodine include lugol's solution, and Tincture of Iodine. Both are solutions in which pure iodine has been dissolved in a solvent of potassium iodide solution. Tincture of Iodine contains some alcohol in addition, but this is not a concern or disadvantage considering the small dosages. Lugol's solution, also known as "strong iodine" solution, was brought to my attention by John Burleson and Merrill Cohen. They both found that it stimulated growth in *Xenia* species, and helped prevent common "crashes" of this soft coral. Interestingly, they both observed that potassium iodide alone did not have the same effect. Lugol's solution is not a common item on the shelf at your local drugstore, but most pharmacies are able to order it for you, if you are patient enough to wait. Tincture of Iodine is available at grocery stores and pharmacies everywhere.

Iodine appears to be essential for the long term maintenance of *Xenia* species and certain algae. It is also beneficial to other soft corals, especially *Anthelia* and "Clove Polyp" (*Clavularia* sp.). Furthermore, I have seen greater expansion of mushroom anemones after a routine of iodine additions has been established, and I have also noticed that iodine is useful for treating infections which occasionally affect zoanthid anemones...it may be administered directly over the colonial anemones(pers. obs.) and over *Xenia* (John Burleson, pers. comm), but not all invertebrates tolerate direct exposure. Too much added to the tank at once may injure the fish and invertebrates,(pers obs, and Mike Paletta, Charles Delbeek pers. comms.), and can stimulate the growth of red Cyanobacteria (Alf Nilsen, pers. comm.). So, a word of caution is in order regarding the dosage. Iodine is very toxic stuff and must not be over-dosed. While the dosage for potassium iodide is known, as I described at the beginning of this discussion, the limits for Lugol's and Tincture of Iodine are less clear. When I use either of these I simply add them over the target organism, be it a *Xenia* sp., or *Dictyota* or *Sargassum* algae. In this way I avoid overdosing the water. Now you're on your own.

Q. Dear Julian,
Let me begin my tale of woe by first stating that I am at my wits end. My problems first started when I decided to trade my old glass 55 gal. salt tank in on a 60 gal acrylic flatback. I transferred the large 5-6" Orbic Batfish, Yellow Tang, 3-stripe Damsel, Yellow Tail Damsel, Blue Damsel, Figure Eight Puffer, and Koran Angel without problem to the new tank. Anticipating a reef in the future, I purchased and installed in the canopy one 48" Philips Actinic 03 40w bulb, one 48" Sylvania Daylight 40w bulb, and a 24" 30 w Triton mounted on cut mirrored plexiglass. About two weeks later the Batfish and Yellow Tang got ick. The puffer caught it within days. I treated with copper sulfate in the tank, and copper formalin baths. The puffer got freshwater baths. All worked, and the tank was soon rid of any trace of ick. I removed the copper with bags of activated carbon in the wet/dry sump.

Approximately 3-4 weeks later I received a Powder Blue Tang, Tasseled Filefish, and Flame Wrasse, along with a large 12" Ritteri Anemone as birthday gifts. The Tasseled Filefish died within a week for unknown reasons. The next week ick struck again and claimed the wrasse and my now prized Powder Blue Tang. Armed with water samples I ran to my two favorite fish stores where I received conflicting testimony. One advised the ick spores had cycled and hatched after 17-21 days and came back harder, while the other store believed some sort of toxin was at work and the ick was caused by the stress of the toxin. Next the Yellow Tail and three-stripe Damsels died. They had no ick or other marks on them and had been eating and behaving fine. I kept the damsels for two years and they were hardy fish. I decided it was time for drastic measures and did a complete tear down. The fish stores were kind enough to keep the remaining fish and anemone for me. I removed all of the off-white quartz gravel and dumped all 60 gallons of water. At this time I also decided to take the plunge and bought seeded live rock to make a reef. I was advised to keep the DLS which I was considering replacing with Bio-balls. I treated the new water with Amquel and used Instant Ocean salt. I ran the wet/dry and protein skimmer for a week and had excellent water quality so I returned the Yellow Tang and Batfish to the tank. The Blue Damsel had died suddenly at the fish store for unknown reasons and the puffer died of ick, also at the fish store. The anemone also died at the other fish store; I was told it "fell apart" after 2 days. I thought this was unusual as it had no tears or punctures and was doing well. A friend gave me five small Percula Clowns as she was getting out of the hobby. Within five days three clowns were dead for unknown reasons, no spots no illness, no nothing. The only peculiarity is each morning the batfish is covered with ick-like spots which disappear by evening. Some spot covered slime can usually be found floating in the tank.

The only clue I can provide to this mystery is I am having some difficulty controlling the temperature. During the day, the lighting heats up the water to approx. 80-82 degrees F. At night this cools to approx 76-78 degrees F. I am buying a fan this week but don't know if it will help or if temperature is even the problem. I cannot think of any way any foreign toxins may have found their way into the tank. My water is currently as follows: salinity - 1.021, pH - 8.3, Nitrate - approx 10ppm., phosphate and water hardness are not problems here. The only additive to the water is Coralife tank cleaner...algae is not a problem. Should I add copper? I have no live corals, inverts, or anemones.(I'm afraid to buy any!) Please help!! Sincerely, Brian Paul, Gaithersburg, Md.

A. Toxin shmoxin, we have a very basic, though very frustrating situation here. The "ick" your fish experienced, at least initially, was *Amyloodinium*, which is many times more fatal than *Cryptocaryon*, the other "white spot" or "ick". Once your fishes' resistance took a beating from the *Amyloodinium*, a secondary bacterial infection, most likely a *Vibrio*, finished them off. *Vibrio* probably took your two year old damsels, as I will explain in a moment.

I am concerned about the bottom media in your tank. As I understand, you have a wet/dry filter...I assume you haven't got an undergravel filter. If you have replaced the quartz gravel, or placed some other gravel on the bottom, how thick is it? If it is thicker than 1/2 inch, and you don't have strong currents or gravel sifting creatures like watchman and sleeper gobies, sea cucumbers, and pistol shrimps, then it is possible that you are developing strongly reducing areas in the bottom, which rob the system of oxygen and may release toxic hydrogen sulfide. This would be a further stress, ok, yes, a toxin of sorts, in addition to the temperature swings. It sounds like you have removed the gravel and left the bottom bare...that's fine. It is possible that you had too much gravel before. But that is not the reason for your woes.

Tell your friends never to buy you live presents again. This is a disastrous practice even if the intentions are good. Friends often haven't a clue about compatibility and the specific requirements of the fish or invertebrates they buy for you. Also, have you ever heard of the practice of quarantine? You would not be "at your wit's end" now if you were more careful about introductions to your aquarium. For the benefit of neophytes reading this column, the old salts of course already know the rules, I will offer some profound wisdom about the nature of the hobby from which we derive so much pleasure.

Rule #1 Fish die.

This fact is something that one must accept completely if one is to derive any pleasure at all from the hobby. It is a fact which can be emotionally devastating... it's really amazing how attached we become to our pets. Nevertheless, despite all our efforts, we cannot remain in control of every aspect of their lives indefinitely. You must always be satisfied that you have done your best, or learn from the mistakes you make and chalk them up to education. Education can be expensive, especially in this hobby!

Rule #2 Fish get sick
It is inevitable, and I'll tell you why...the reason is...

Rule #3 All fish carry pathogens at all times. ie. "there is no such thing as a disease free fish".
A while back there was a booklet available to hobbyists which explained a series of quarantine steps to assure pathogen-free fish. This heroic publication seemed to assert that this was the only way to go. Actually, if you are patient enough to take steps to quarantine fish and treat for specific diseases, as all public aquaria do, your chances of disease outbreak in a closed system are dramatically reduced...though this is only partly owing to the eradication of the parasites. Most significant, in my opinion, is that the quarantine period affords the fish a chance to acclimate to the captive environment and artificial food sources, enabling them to regain their strength and immunity which have been weakened by the stresses of capture and handling. What's good about the quarantine method is that the fish don't have the added stress of battling over established territories with resident fish, and the water is treated so that most incidences of disease are easily managed...not the case, as you discovered Brian, when the fish are just dumped right in. As you become more skilled, it is likely that you will become more foolish and impatient (this includes yours truly, folks), but at least your skill affords you an added feature over plain dumb luck, so you may get away without quarantine...this doesn't mean that you should ultimately strive to be foolish, however. If your goal is long term gratification, be patient and quarantine the fish.

I think it is misleading when reef-keeping hobbyists claim that such tanks are naturally disease resistant. It is unfortunately true that these aquaria, by virtue of their more perfect simulation of the marine environment, and perhaps additional pathogen reducing benefits from certain plants and invertebrates, actually do lower the incidence of disease. It is unfortunate because there are no guarantees on the safety margin, and the foolhardy "dump the fish in" attitude totally ignores some of the less common, but chronically destructive diseases like trematodes and flukes, in deference to the common threat of ick, which is often easy to control.

Amyloodinium is a type of ick which can really run a terrible course through the fish population, even in a reef tank, where its occurrence is most frustrating because treatment is basically impossible without removing the fish. *Cryptocaryon*, on the other hand, generally goes away when the temperature is stabilized, especially when the salinity is lowered as well...I'm pretty sure by your description of the disappearing-reappearing spots, that your batfish now suffers from *Cryptocaryon*.

Secondary *Vibrio* infections are typically the fatal blow after the initial insult by the parasites. Even when fish build up an immunity to *Cryptocaryon* or *Amyloodinium*, the stress of fighting off tremendous quantities of these parasites when other, less resistant fish break down with the disease, often produces a fatal systemic infection, as happened to your Damselfishes.

On the subject of immunity, certain fish have higher ability to resist "ick" than others. Hawkfishes and Damselfishes, for the most part, are really tough and capable of avoiding trouble with "ick". Most surgeonfishes or "tangs", however have very low resistance to ick. They are "ick fish". Powder Blue tangs are really terrible in this regard, as you noticed. They should always be quarantined, in my opinion.You said your tank now has live rock in it, so copper treatment is not the thing to do. You need to slow down and begin to take control of the situation, Brian. First, the temperature swings you mentioned are the most common chronic stress which contributes to the incidence of "ick"...temperature is a large part of the problem.

Although I would prefer to maintain the aquarium at a cooler temperature, 82 degrees is not too bad for a fish tank, so you might consider installing a good heater to maintain that temperature at night when the lights are off. If you can afford it, the best option for temperature control is a chiller/heater combination.

It is not necessary for you to tear your tank down again in the nearly impossible quest of a completely pathogen free tank. Rather, it is now time to stabilize the environment, and allow the resident fish to fight off the disease on their own or die. Don't run out and buy new fish as soon as the coast looks clear. Be patient, and by all means quarantine your next additions, ok?

While we're on the subject of disease, hoo boy can we possibly have another endorsement here? Well, Don sent me a copy for review of this fantastic new computer guide to fish care and disease prevention, diagnosis, and treatment, called "Professor Fish." By the looks of your letter, Brian, I think you have a computer, and I know that you would learn a lot from this program... I wish the stores you frequent had the program running to explain to customers (and employees) how to avoid fish "death for unknown reasons". That being said, my review will appear soon.

Next month, lots of letters answered for sure.

December 1991

Before answering your questions this month, I wanted to give you a little something to think about, in the form of an analogy. It concerns the fate of the marine life collector, here in Florida, and elsewhere. It seems as if the government and many so-called "environmental" groups are picking an easy target, aiming to eliminate the few who harvest the fruits of the trees, and ignoring the many who set the fires which burn them down. Talk about not being able to see the forest for the trees!

How does this affect you, the consumer? Frankly, you are targeted as well. In the fury of environmental emotionalism, people in power are missing a very important issue. The seeds harvested by the marine life fisherman are a renewable resource. The marine life fisherman's harvest, planted in your aquarium, affords you and everyone who sees your little ocean, the full appreciation of the beauty, frailty, and wonder of life in the sea. You learn from the seeds he harvests, and your garden eventually flourishes so that you too can offer seeds to others. I contend that without this channel of awareness, exposure, and education, we will never understand how to cope with the forces which really impact and destroy the reefs. As a consequence, the general population won't even care because it will never really know the reef's beauty and significance. I also contend that leaving the right to study captive reefs in the hands of a few "authorized" scientists is very wrong. As a scientist myself, I know that most scientists, of necessity, view their area of expertise through a sort of "tunnel vision" in order to specialize in the particular area which either interests them or provides enough grant money to keep them going. Furthermore, I have seen that being a good scientist has no bearing on one's ability to be a good aquarist. Knowledge helps you if you already have a green thumb, but it won't give you one. Having thousands of aquarists observing reefs in their homes affords everyone a far better potential for significant discovery, than if the privilege belonged to only a few scientists who can't understand why they have no success with one species so they avoid it and spend the rest of their career on a hardy one. Or, they try and try again without changing the parameters which caused the failure in the first place because they know that their hypothetical model is correct. Most aquarists are more flexible and open minded than this, and so their observations are certainly valuable, especially considering their numbers. Aquarium hobbyists are succeeding in the cultivation of species of marine life that are known to produce useful pharmaceuticals for the treatment of human disease. I believe that the published work of aquarists who specialize in cultivation techniques is as valuable as the work of any marine scientist, and the marine scientists could certainly benefit from keeping up with aquarium publications and journals.

I write this now because I feel really frustrated when I hear rumors that the supply of live corals will eventually be cut off. I am discouraged when I hear "environmentalists" spew out emotional testimony against the collection of marine life, without a whit of supporting scientific evidence to suggest that any harm or significant impact is done by this endeavor, and see that their testimony is what the deciding officials really want to hear. And I wonder how, in a Democratic society, the deciding officials can come to a decision without your input.
Sitting on my desk at the moment is a copy of a page from the Federal Register, Vol. 58, No. 158, that I

received from Dr. Paul Loiselle, in which NOAA (the National Oceanic and Atmospheric Administration) announces that it received a petition for emergency rule making or fishery management plan action under the Magnuson Fishery Conservation and Management Act. Basically, the U.S. Department of Commerce and the National Marine Fisheries Service have been petitioned to proclaim a rule prohibiting the taking and landing of live rock within the agency's jurisdiction for the South Atlantic, Caribbean, and Gulf of Mexico. I ask you, what do these people really know about live rock? What gives them the ability to make their decision? The petitioner is an environmental group, ironically called "Project Reefkeeper!" The NMFS is accepting comments to determine whether to proceed with the regulations suggested by the petition . . . these comments were accepted until September 30, 1991. You're too late folks, and I couldn't have informed you in time anyway, considering the three month lag time of a commercial publication such as this. Still. I suspect (okay, okay, I hope) that your input even at a late date can have an impact.
Please write to:

> B. Michael McLemore, Attorney Advisor,
> Office of General Counsel, NOAA.
> 9450 Koger Boulevard, Suite I 18,
> St. Petersburg, Florida 33702,
> (813) 893-3817.

As the events of this situation unfold, I will have more to say for sure. I hope that the collective voice of FAMA's readership will make its concern known. Please read an editorial on this subject by Charles Delbeek, for additional information.

Q. Dear Mr. Sprung.
Last week I accidentally overdosed my 55-gallon reef tank with 30 times the recommr?nded daily dosage of Iodine with (so far) no adverse effect! I did not realize what I had done until the next day. Since there did not seem to he any problems, I did not take any drastic measures but added an extra Polyfilter® and bag of Chemi-Pure® after my usual weekly 5 gallon water change as a

precaution. The overdose has not seemed to have any ill effect on the water quality as far as I can tell, or the live-stock (4 small damsels, a yellow tang, four hard corals --- *Goniopora*, Bubble, Plate, and Grape --- soft corals, giant carpet anemone, 75 pounds of live rock with attendant "critters" and about 18 snails).

Needless to say, I do not intend to add any additional iodine for at least 30 days and will never again use any new product when I'm too tired to think straight. I am curious (and relieved) that the overdose did not have the dire consequence that Moe and Thiel seem to warn about, and would very much appreciate your advice as to what steps, if any, I should take to prevent possible problems arising from the overdose. Is it possible that the tank was so depleted of iodine that it absorbed the apparent overdose without problem? Should I increase the water changes to dilute excess iodine? If so, by how much and how often? Moe notes that algae absorbs iodine. Should I add some now to absorb the excess iodine? Sincerely, Michael P. Enright Brooklyn, New York

P.S.. I have also begun adding a drop of iodine and 4 ounces of Kalkwasser daily to my 45 gallon "convention-al" tank (filtered with 3 canisters filled with bio media or carbon and a protein skimmer) for the benefit of the macro-algae (*Caulerpa* and *Halimeda*). The tank also has two Royal Grammas, which I hope to breed, and an assortment of small crabs, shrimp, anemones, and urchins. Will the macroalgae & invertebrates benefit from the iodine and Kalkwasser? Since there is no sump, is it okay to add the Kalkwasser directly to the tank? Thanks once again for your help.

A. Well, Michael, it looks like you were lucky. I'm not sure what type of iodine you are using or what strength it is, so I can't really judge just how much of an overdose you administered. No, you should not "add algae," and no, the tank did not absorb the iodine because of defi-ciency. A water change would have been a good idea, considering the suspected overdose. But now, however, considering the absence of any harmful effect, my best advice to you is don't worry . . . there's no problem, just don't do it again. Protein skimming, by the way, does remove some iodine.

On the subject of your postscript, yes, of course the algae and inverts will benefit from your addition of Iodine and Kalkwasser. Adding pure Kalkwasser directly to the tank is a little risky because of its high pH. If you have a CO_2 system to counteract the pH rise that results from this addition, then there's no problem. Also, the risk of adding Kalkwasser depends on the volume of the tank, the volume of Kalkwasser added, and the biomass of life producing CO_2 as it is added. I can assure you that four ounces of Kalkwasser added to a 45 gallon tank daily is completely safe . . . you may just pour it right in, though be sure that you add it in the flow of water to mix it. If, for example, you were adding something like half a gallon or more to this tank, you would not do it all at once; rather, it would be best added via a dosing pump or a drip system. If the Kalkwasser is added at night, after the lights have gone off, there is more CO_2 available to counter the initial pH rise.

Q. Dear Julian:
I enjoyed the opportunity to speak with you and to listen to your great presentation at MACNA3. I have two questions for your Reef Notes column: (1) Have you determined why the reef tanks in your presentation all have a substrate on the bottom? (2) Would you please give us an update on your personal tank?
Regards, Joseph E. Oskowiak,
Abington, PA

A. Thanks, Joe. It seems the tanks all had a substrate on the bottom because their owners put one there. First, for the benefit of the readers who did not attend MACNA, the photos Joe is referring to were taken by Alf Jacob Nilsen in Norway and in Germany, in 1985 and 1990. They demonstrated reproducible success withgrowing stony corals using protein skimming and good quality live rock. The bottom media in these tanks varied from coral sand to small, gravel-sized pieces of live rock. When I visited Alf in Norway in August of 1990, I saw several very nice aquariums established this way, and often the sand on the bottom was quite thick . . . an inch or more in some areas. I believe I explained this at MACNA, but perhaps because of the time constraint I didn't offer the complete picture. What these tanks had in common was the use of small pistol shrimps (*Alpheus* and *Synalpheus sp.*), and the gobies: *Cryptocentrus cinctus, C. leptocephalus,* also known as "watchmen gobies", two or three types of *Amblygobius sp.,* and *Valenciennea strigata,* the yellow headed sleeper. These all constantly sift through the sand in search of food, and thus keep it swept clean. In addition, the tanks had small sea cucumbers which also sort (and "eat") the sand. All of the tanks I saw had very strong water motion provided by several Turbelle powerheads controlled with an automatic switching device to simulate wave surges . . . this also helps to keep the bottom clean by preventing the formation of "dead spots" in the water flow where detritus could settle out. I think these hobbyists choose to put a substrate on the bottom primarily for aesthetic reasons, but there is one other significant advantage to having a substrate, and I have mentioned this before in my column. When there is a substrate on the bottom, it affords a sort of refuge for copepods and amphipods to multiply and provide a continuous food source to the fishes. In a substrate-free tank these crustaceans maintain much lower populations because the fish are able to seek them out more readily. Charles Delbeek received some indication from Dietrich Stüber, whose aquarium was also featured at MACNA, that he has found a chemical reason for including large gravel chunks on the bottom of his aquarium. The gravel in this tank is coated by pink coralline algae, and appears like small pieces of live rock. Stüber seemed to indicate that the gravel was important for buffering, but I suspect either that he meant something else. . . possibly something was lost in the translation from German, or that he was mistaken.*

*I have since learned that the presence of a bottom substrate tends to prevent depletion of alkalinity. This works several ways. Dissolution of the calcium carbonate by CO_2 is only part of the reason. Breakdown of organic detritus generates CO_2 and carbonates, also contributing to alkalinity. This occurs as part of the denitrification process mediated by bacteria.

I have recommended substrate-free reef tanks primarily to teach beginning hobbyists about detritus accumulation and the importance of removing it from the system. Without a substrate, the detritus is easy to see and siphon out. This does not mean that I have any negative impression of a tank with a substrate. On the contrary, when it's done right this is an admirable feat. As far as

Depending on the depth of the substrate and water circulation, the use of larger grains could be beneficial in the sense that it might simulate the isolated water/ diffusion effect created by a plenum in Jaubert's system. See volume one of this series for a detailed description.

**I still have this reef aquarium, but now it does have a substrate (live sand) on the bottom. In subsequent Reef Notes I describe my experiences with adding sand to this aquarium.

***In Jaubert's system (see volume one of this series) a protein skimmer may be used, but it is not always used. Bacteria in the sand can break down dissolved organic compounds. When there is heavy feeding, however, the system really requires protein skimming to maintain the nutrient poor condition.

aesthetics go, some hobbyists prefer the look of sand on the bottom, and some do not. If you don't have sand on the bottom, then encrusting soft corals and anemones, as well as small pieces of live rock create a nice effect.

Regarding my own aquarium, I still have the 15 gallon tank. It is beautiful, and it still has no substrate on the bottom . . . you can see it in my new video, if I may make a plug. I have added an external pump to flush behind the reef and sweep detritus out, and I have also added an automatic water make-up system using Kalkwasser only.**

I am presently setting up a 60 gallon reef tank, a two foot by two foot by two foot cube, in which the reef will be built in the center and viewable from all sides, and the bottom will be live coral sand which I will collect in the vicinity of a coral reef, and there will be *Thalassia* sea grass seedlings planted in it. I have already successfully established a tank with nearly four inches of live sand and sea grass in a private home, and this tank's beauty has inspired me to make one at home. . . which is always a long process, it seems.

You may sense a change of heart on my part regarding the use of substrate, but actually this is not so. These successful aquaria, in addition to using biological means of keeping the substrate clean, were also incorporating another important element. . . they all strictly maintained a nutrient poor environment through the use of protein skimming and filtered make-up water free of phosphate or nitrate. Without these elements, their success would be sacrificed, as the substrate acts sort of like a sponge, absorbing phosphate which can be liberated at times, causing uncontrollable algae growth, as I have pointed out in the past. So, to clarify, successful aquaria using sand or gravel on the bottom need to be maintained in a nutrient poor condition through careful prevention of nutrient accumulation. This is accomplished by limiting nutrient sources, and using animals which prevent the build-up of nutrient-rich detritus in the system through their substrate-sifting behavior. Establishing and maintaining these aquaria is not difficult, and I encourage you to try it.***

I hope we all will continue to have the opportunity to create and study reefs at home. This opportunity depends on the level-headed input and involvement of concerned hobbyists like you.

January 1992

Q. Dear Mr. Sprung,
I have a 110 gallon reef aquarium serviced by a dual chamber wet/dry filter outfitted with spray bars and containing bioballs. There is no media, other than a sponge filter in the wet section. I constantly run an exterior protein skimmer which is 36 inches tall and operates properly. Additionally, I run an ozone reactor and redox controller. The prefilter and sump sponge are cleaned regularly. Water exiting the reactor is flowed over carbon, which is also changed regularly. Lighting is provided by two 5500K metal halide bulbs and an actinic 03 and daylight fluorescent. There is no substrate in the tank and rock is elevated above the tank floor on eggcrate. Water is returned at the top of the tank and below the eggcrate in an attempt to keep the bottom clean. Additional circulation is provided by two powerheads which alternate at 45 second intervals.

Base rock in the tank is primarily of the "tufa" type. Florida and Hawaiian live rock are also used. The tank contains various corals including elegance coral, grape coral, mushroom coral, and lettuce coral. The tank also contains a Ritteri anemone, a Humma Humma trigger, a Hippo Tang, a Sebae Clown, a Yellow Tang and a Kole tang. Redox is maintained between 390 and 440 millivolts. Nitrate levels are below 0.25, as measured by a reputable kit. Additionally phosphate levels are zero. Dkh is 10. Calcium is adequate. Strontium and Molybdenum are added. All water added to the tank is reverse osmosis treated. The tank has been running for about two years.

In the past months I have been plagued by an insurmountable growth of hair algae. I have reduced lighting periods, increased water changes, changed salts, added *Turbo* snails, added tangs, utilized different filter elements, tried water additives, cut back on feeding of fish, eliminated feeding of corals and removed all rock and

cleaned it. Nothing seems to stop my "wonderful" hair algae growth. I am told the cause is possibly an increased level of D.O.C.'s (dissolved organic compounds) or phosphorous. What exactly are these? If these are present, must nitrate and phosphate also be present? Are they the likely cause of my problem? If so, how do I eliminate them? I am beginning to believe that if you have strong lighting in the reef tank, there is no way around hair algae.
Very truly yours,
Edmund E. Gibbs,
Highland Mills, N.Y.

A. Well, Ed, this good long letter deserves a long answer. There are several valuable points brought out by your questions and descriptions, and the solutions I will explain should help everyone willing to follow my advice. Judging by your description, it sounds like you've reviewed my past comments about hair algae... I won't rehash them, but will stick to the circumstances producing the growth in your tank.

First, let me state that your assumption about strong lighting inevitably causing unmanageable algae is wrong...aren't you relieved? This means that I can help you, but you will have to make some changes, which means it's going to take a little work and some patience.

Also, if the trigger fish is like a favorite pet, I suggest you set up another tank for it. Otherwise, take him back and trade him for a piece of live coral or something. Triggerfish eat a lot, a characteristic we don't want in fishes for the reef tank unless they are herbivores. Also, yours will ultimately munch on something you don't want him to, so the sooner he's out the better.

By your description it sounds like you've spent a lot of time and money on your system, and that you have received a lot of good advice along the way...that's good, but there are some problems, and possible problems, which are contributing to the real problem hair algae. Most notable is that you have used dead base rock to build your reef. A few pieces here and their to prop up a specimen or live rock is ok, but when dead rock is used as the principle base structure, hair algae is difficult to avoid. Hair algae "likes" to grow on bare limestone rocks, like tufa, and perpetuates its presence on these rocks by trapping nutrient rich detritus in the network of its tangled filaments. Also, the porous structure of tufa tends to trap detritus and encourages algae growth. Live rocks have encrusting coralline algae growing on them which effectively retard the growth of hair algae on the rock. If the corallines die, and bare limestone is exposed, the hair algae has a chance to gain a foothold, but it may not since there are also tiny flea-like crustaceans called amphipods which live on the rocks and come out at night to graze on algae.

To maintain good growth of coralline algae, you need to maintain a calcium level of at least 400mg/l, a hardness of 7 dkh or higher, and keep up with strontium additions. You indicated an "adequate" calcium level , but didn't give me the opportunity to judge, nor did you indicate how you maintain the level. Ideally, you should be making kalkwasser by adding a teaspoon of calcium hydroxide or calcium oxide to each gallon of your make-up water, and adding this solution slowly to the tank by means of an automatic water make-up system or by a drip system. Please see my past columns and the list of references for more detailed information and cautions about calcium additions and measurement. I don't know which calcium test kit you are using, and whether you are using the correct conversion factor to calculate the measured value... please refer to my column on this subject.

If you really want to finally lick the hair algae problem, I'm afraid you will have to take the reef apart again, remove most or all of the tufa rock, and reassemble the reef loosely stacked with new live rock. This change must be done properly, of course. The new live rock should be held in a separate aquarium or container with good circulation and maintained between 70 and 80 degrees Farenheight for at least three weeks to allow any fouling to be cleansed away by the resident bacteria and microorganisms. If you don't hold and "cure" it first this way, you risk killing off the inhabitants of your aquarium.

You mentioned snails, Edmund, but not how many you had. I recommend that you try both *Turbo* and *Astraea* snails. The *Turbo*'s are larger and hungrier, so you can use fewer of them, but *Astraea* snails are best employed at a concentration of one per gallon. If you already have some *Turbo* snails, then you don't need quite this many *Astraea*'s. When you have high concentrations of these herbivores, even the glass stays clean. All the while these little scrubbers graze, they produce little fecal pellets. Therefore, in a tank like yours where detritus is regularly removed from the system, snails are an efficient means of maintaining the nutrient poor condition. Your use of both the yellow *Zebrasoma* tang and the Kole tang is ideal...keep them. Also, the conservative approach to food additions to the aquarium is good policy... don't pollute!*

*Two points I want to mention here. First, I neglected to mention tiny hermit crabs as a good control for filamentous algae. They are very good grazers, and can be included at one or two per gallon, with fewer snails needed. (see volume one of this series and *The Reef Aquarium* Volume One). Second, when nutrient control is managed via protein skimming and denitrification in the substrates, feeding is BENEFICIAL to the system. It is not healthy to run an anorexic tank!

Finally, while it's true that an ozone reactor (a.k.a. oxygen reactor) is an efficient means of elevating redox potential, and that it improves the water quality through oxidation of pollutants, I think your system would be better off with a second protein skimmer instead. It has been my experience that in the long run it is better to remove these pollutants by skimming than to simply oxidize them. The skimmer would be easy to install in the place of the oxygen reactor.

Each of the points I have touched upon has a subtle but important contribution to the problem hair algae now plaguing your reef tank. I want to see you become satisfied with your aquarium in the long run...don't let the green hair discourage you, I'm sure you will beat it.

Oh, look, Ethel, another one of those letters with "just one question"...

Q. Dear Julian,
First I would like to thank you for all of the information I have gotten from your Reef Notes column. I'm sure I am one of many who have benefitted greatly from your articles.

I have only one question that I would like to ask you about. I am currently piecing together a 110 gallon reef system. I have looked in great detail at the "American" method of reef tanks which I look at as, if a problem exists, add another piece of equipment. Every now and then I am teased by the pictures in magazines of tanks following the "Berlin School" of reef keeping and am amazed at how beautiful they are. I then read on and find out the following basics are in common with them:

1. Protein skimming-usually a larger unit than in USA.
2. No Wet/Dry
3. H.Q.I. lighting, usually 250 w Osram Power Stars
4. Addition of Calcium and Strontium.
5. High quality live rock.
6. R.O. or D.I. water used for water replacement.
7. Very good water circulation to eliminate dead spots

This is great except for one thing. Not enough information to set a tank up with. So my one question just got larger. Can you fill in some of these gaps well enough for me to get started, for example.

1. Are wet/dry units removed after the rock has cycled or are they never installed?

2. Mechanical filtration is never mentioned-any thoughts on this aspect?

3. I have a lot of doubt about the existence of Poly Filters, X - Nitrate, and X - Phosphate in Europe, what about these problems? I am assuming they don't exist but have not been able to find a reason why.

4. Is activated carbon used? I have seen where someone was using it four to five days a month and then removing it.

5. Water changes aren't documented well either. I have heard that they are much smaller than what is considered normal here.

6. Ozone use is also unmentioned. I am assuming the redox is naturally very high...is this correct?

I realize that these are a lot of points, but they are ones I

have never seen anything on. They also seem relatively important and should not be left out. The system I'm going to set up will be almost exclusively corals with the majority hard corals. I plan on keeping only a couple of fish to keep the algae in check somewhat.
Thanks again,
Roger W. Williams,
Clinton, N.J.

A. I know that much of this information has been covered in articles about the Berlin method, Roger, but perhaps the definition hasn't been distinguished so numerically, and people missed it. I have heard your questions many times since the publication of these articles, and I'm glad you wrote and gave me the opportunity to specifically address these points...but next time don't try to fool me with the "one question" routine.

1. Wet/Dry units are not installed in the first place. The live rock is added to the aquarium and allowed to "cure," which may take three weeks or longer. Patience is emphasized. The longer you wait before adding fishes, the more developed the populations of tiny crustaceans and other microfauna become. The first fish added should be herbivores. No harm is done by installing a wet/dry filter and then removing it, but there is no advantage to doing this either. The rock will foul and cure whether such a filter is present or not.

2. I definitely wrote about mechanical filtration. It is definitely used as an important means of maintaining the nutrient poor condition. As I explained in the previous answer, herbivores such as snails and tangs produce fecal pellets as they graze away the algae growth. The algae strip the nutrients nitrogen and phosphate out of the water, and as the herbivores graze, they encourage more algae growth. If you have good mechanical filtration combined with good circulation, their nutrient rich fecal pellets are easily removed from the system. The prefilter used in the wet/dry systems here works well as a mechanical filter unit when a fine media is used to trap the detritus particles. Such fine media also traps some amino acids and proteins, which means it removes

*A change of opinion here. I later learned that these filter cartridges were installed temporarily and usually not used on a continuous basis. I began experimenting with running my reef aquaria without mechanical filtration and discovered that the protein skimmer pulled out more "gunk" and I had eliminated a maintenance chore. I do periodically install a mechanical filter and blast the reef with a powerhead to blow out settled detritus. I also siphon detritus out of the sump once or twice per year.

**In fact that is no longer the case. Charles Delbeek visited with aquarists there and found that the trend had changed in the time since George Smit presented his series in FAMA magazine about Dutch "Miniriffs." Many aquarists there have eliminated the lush growth of plants in favor of soft and stony corals.

***Actually nitrate can accumulate in these

potential sources of nitrogen in the system when cleaned regularly. BIG CAUTION: if you use a fine media in the prefilter chamber, be sure that its rapid clogging won't prevent water from flowing through the unit... this would cause your aquarium to overflow, of course. I use plain old filter floss for mechanical filtration...I hope you weren't imagining some new high-tech media designed specifically for the reef keeping hobbyist. For safety, you could install a mechanical filter in the sump, where the dry section used to be. This could make cleaning easier and would prevent the possibility of overflowing your tank. Many European hobbyists use Turbelle powerheads in their aquaria with attached Tunze prefilter cartridges, and they clean these often as well.*

3. I don't doubt that the products you mentioned are in use in Europe, which brings up another issue. Europeans have not simply thrown away the wet/dry idea, nor have they thrown away undergravel filters. In the Netherlands, where reef aquariums emphasize a lot of plant growth, wet/dry filters are definitely the popular choice.** Even in Germany, where this method was born, there is still popular use of wet/dry filtration and oxygen reactors on reef aquariums. One must accept that there is still and will always be great diversity of opinion and practice in Europe and elsewhere, hence the name "Berlin School" for the method you are specifically asking about. This method was developed by a handful of hobbyists trying to optimize captive growth of stony corals. Now the method is well accepted, and has spread primarily in Germany, Switzerland, and Norway, and I think many hobbyists here in North America are catching on as well. Now, regarding your specific question number three, nitrate does not accumulate in these aquaria, because most of its sources are quickly eliminated from the system before they can be oxidized to nitrate.*** When an aquarium has a wet/dry filter and surface skimming overflow, the combination makes for a very efficient nitrate factory. You see, surface skimmed water contains attached surface active amino acids and proteins, rich in nitrogen. These are passed over the filter media constantly, a fact which rapidly encourages the growth of heterotrophic bacteria that convert the proteins and

aquaria when there is
not sufficient denitrifi-
cation ocurring in the
sand or live rocks.

****Denitrification in
the rocks and sand can
also reduce this
nitrate.

*****The use of kalk-
wasser also helps to
control phosphate lev-
els. When kalkwasser
is regularly adminis-
tered to the aquarium
phosphate precipitates
and the level of dis-
solved phosphate in the
water remains very low.

******See Craig
Bingman's article about
carbon and light trans-
mission in *Aquarium
Frontiers*, Summer 1995
issue.

amino acids into ammonia, which encourages the growth of *Nitrosomonas* bacteria that convert the ammonia to nitrite, which encourages the growth of *Nitrobacter* bacteria that convert the nitrite to nitrate, and this oxidation process is greatly enhanced by the high saturation of oxygen within the filter. Good protein skimming used in combination with the wet/dry filter reduces the potential conversion of nitrogen rich compounds into nitrate, and small fish populations and limited feeding also reduce this potential. Thus a wet/dry filter does not always cause a chronic nitrate problem, but it can easily do so when no protein skimming is employed and a lot of food is going into the system.****

Phosphate is kept low by the use of good circulation and mechanical filtration as I explained a moment ago, and through the use of purified make-up water and protein skimming.***** When all of these practices are employed, there is no need for products which absorb phosphate.

4. Activated carbon is used to keep the water crystal clear, which enhances light transmission. Hobbyists differ in opinion over which brand is best and how often to use it. You will have to experiment with this one and decide for yourself.******

5. Water changes, frequency and size, also fall under the category of opinion, though many hobbyists practicing the Berlin method seem to agree that smaller water changes are less disturbing to the invertebrates. I generally recommend about 25% a month for beginning hobbyists, though I know that many successful reef aquaria are maintained with water changes of less than 10% per month, with some of that being the replacement of water skimmed off by the protein skimmer.

6. The use of a lot of ozone is counter to the practice of protein skimming...that is, it prevents skimming by oxidizing compounds that the skimmer would remove. For this reason ozone is not generally used under normal operating conditions in the Berlin method. However, it is typical for these aquaria to have a redox controller and ozonizer installed to boost the redox in the extreme

event of some accidental death causing extra water pollution. Some hobbyists employ continuous use of ozone in low doses, which does not interfere with skimming and has a slight germicidal effect.

I hope you are comfortable enough with these answers to go out and get started on building the perfect coral garden.

February 1992

I just spent two nice weekends with the Potomac Valley Aquarium Society and with the Cleveland Saltwater Enthusiasts Association... saw some interesting aquariums, met some really nice people, had sushi both weekends, caught the peak of the fall color display, and was reminded by my sinuses why the tropical heat is essential for my longterm survival.

Q. Dear Julian,
I would like to find out about the affects of an ozonizer versus an oxygenator filled with activated hydrogen peroxide, which is in a bottle and has a catalyst in it which releases a certain amount. I've heard both can be dangerous, should I use either or neither? I have a 190 gallon reef system, with a wet/dry and a counter current protein skimmer. Please help, I've heard horror stories about both. Also, do you need a deionizer or an oxygen/ozone reactor? What is best to use, if any?
Sincerely,
Eddie Humphrey,
Oklahoma City, OK

A. Get a hold of yourself Eddie! If you've heard horror stories then what attraction is there for you? It sounds to me like you've been hearing similar sounding names that you are unfamiliar with, and you've been getting confused. An ozonizer is a device which generates ozone from the oxygen in the air pumped through it. Ozone, the unstable union of three oxygen atoms, readily breaks down to the stable union of two oxygen atoms, while the third oxygen atom "burns" or oxidizes any of a variety of compounds with which it combines. Ozone is used to treat the water for purification. Its oxidizing capability affords a germicidal affect, and it also renders the water crystal clear as water-staining organic compounds are oxidized and broken down. Ozone is never administered directly to the tank, but is applied either in a protein skimmer or a reactor chamber. In either of these the ozone contacts the water and purifies it, and then the residual ozone and potentially noxious oxidized organic compounds are removed from the water by passing it over a bed of activated carbon before returning the water to the tank.

Hydrogen peroxide works similarly to ozone in that it too has an unstable union with an extra oxygen atom. It readily breaks down into its components, water and an extra atom of oxygen. Directly administering hydrogen peroxide to the aquarium to raise the water quality or the dissolved oxygen content is very risky for novices, though some hobbyists have worked out methods of safe administration. I will not offer any recipes here as I do not wish to encourage anyone to play with hydrogen peroxide additions. The Oxygenator you mentioned, Eddie, releases only oxygen bubbles as I understand it. It might seem like a good idea to use one on a reef tank, to elevate the dissolved oxygen concentration, but it is not. It rapidly produces a very high supersaturation level of dissolved oxygen, which is toxic to many invertebrates. The oxygenator is beneficial for fish tanks, especially heavily stocked ones, and perhaps freshwater planted aquariums in which the oxygen level may fall really low at night.

Deionizer is a name which may sound a lot like ozonizer, but the two are very different. A deionizer purifies the freshwater that you use as make-up for evaporation, or to mix your saltwater. The deionizer is often used in combination with a mechanical filter which traps particulate matter, and an activated carbon filter. You should be using either a deionizer or a reverse osmosis filter, or both to purify the water you add to your reef tank.

Q. Dear Julian,
I am concerned regarding the continuous ozone smell from my 200 gallon aquarium that I just moved down to my basement. I have tried to find out if there is any evidence of ozone toxicity to humans after prolonged exposure. I am concerned especially for young children

whose lungs may not be totally developed yet. I contacted a physician of occupational medicine who faxed me some studies and references. As the conclusion is still unclear to me, I will shut off my ozonizer until I will be reassured of no toxicity.

I have enclosed copies of articles and references. I would appreciate it if you could comment on ozone toxicity (chronic exposure). As the use of ozonizers is becoming more and more popular, I am quite sure that many readers will find it interesting.
Sincerely Yours,
Emanuele V. Morso, M.D.,
River Grove, IL.

A. Well, Dr. Morso, I cannot reassure you that there is nothing to worry about... your documentation clearly indicates that long term exposure to high levels of ozone does pose a significant health risk. I certainly appreciate the documentation you sent me, but I see no point in scaring or discouraging people about ozone use by describing the potential health hazard, because really it is a very simple matter to install the ozone contact chamber, be it a skimmer or reactor, in such a way as to prevent the escape of any ozone into the room. You smelled ozone in your basement because it was passing freely into the air from the top of your protein skimmer. I don't know what type of skimmer you are using, so I cannot recommend an exact design for you, but in the general sense, you can make one of two types of modifications to eliminate the problem of ozone getting into your living space. You may drill and tap the foam collection cup, and attach ozone tolerating hose (ie. silicone hose) so that you can vent the ozone to the great outdoors (through a window or hole in the wall), and contribute to the air pollution index in your neighborhood. Imagine watching the news when the weatherman reports: "Air quality index today was 18, which is in the good range, with an exception around a Dr. Morso's residence, where we found an unusually high concentration of ozone..."
Next thing you know, the ozone patrol pulls up and you're locked up for five to ten buddy for ozonating without a license. Another option is to drill and tap the

collection cup and, with silicone hose again, attach a container filled with activated carbon which will filter the ozone out of the air passing through. I have seen such containers available commercially, so you may find them at your local pet store, but you can easily build something like this yourself.

I anticipate a few questions which you are bound to have now that you may be contemplating the creation of such a carbon chamber. Basically, if you are concerned about the size of this chamber, one to two liters is plenty. An old canister filter or one of those handy containers for storing food, which you can buy at any supermarket, will serve the purpose. The carbon should be changed as often as necessary to prevent the smell of ozone in the room from occurring...this will probably be several months for a large chamber. Of course you could combine both the carbon chamber and venting to the great outdoors. Finally the material you use for this chamber may become brittle with time and exposure to the ozone, though this deterioration is clearly slowed by the removal of ozone by the activated carbon. The point is that it is not necessary to search for the ultimate, ozone resistant stuff to make a carbon air filter chamber, but it is important to remember that the chamber may become brittle in time.

If you are using an oxygen reactor for ozone contact, a canister filter filled with carbon, plumbed in line after the reactor, will prevent ozone from entering the aquarium and the room. That carbon should be changed about every two months.

Q. Dear Julian,
In the spring of 91 I purchased a giant clam, *Tridacna derasa*. The clam was growing and doing fine, but in June I lost it. The only thing I could pin it down to was the temperature, which was 86 degrees farenheight in the daytime for some days and about 81 degrees at night. I use live rock, carbon, and protein skimming for filtration. The aquarium is a 180 gallon with three 175w 5500K metal halide lamps. Strontium and calcium are the only supplements I am adding. In your opinion,

could temperature have been the problem?

Thanks, Elgie Long, Streator, IL

A. Yes, it certainly could have been the temperature. Giant clams are really very hardy and grow nicely for years, but when something isn't right with them, you know it because they don't open up, and they have the most devastating habit of dying within a few hours. When a clam doesn't look happy, it's time to take immediate action to correct what's bothering it, and this may simply entail removing it from the aquarium and isolating it in another tank for several days, but there are numerous reasons why a clam may bite the dust, some of which I will briefly cover here.

Temperature is critical for all marinelife, especially marine invertebrates from coral reefs. Ideally the temperature should be stable, below 80 degrees farenheight, and above 70 degrees. Your tank was both too warm and the temperature was fluctuating. You mentioned no fish in your aquarium. Perhaps they've been getting sick from the temperature changes. You should consider a chiller and heater combination to maintain your reef and investment.

Fishes often like to supplement the diet you offer with a little clam meat, and even when the nips are only occasional, this can weaken the clam to infection. *Centropyge* spp. angels especially may nip a clam to death, but this is not always so. The beautiful twinspot wrasse likes to dive right in through the clam's incurrent siphon and bite off a hunk of gill or mantle. Clams don't like this very much. Keep a close watch on your fish's behavior... sometimes they resort to clam nipping only when they are really hungry, and feeding them will stop this behavior. Perhaps the fish don't even like clam, but are so smart that they know that all it takes is a few nibbles to bring you running back with lots of food. Ever wonder who's got who trained?

There are some invertebrates which pester giant clams.

*Small bristle worms often attack clams resting on the sand bottom. They enter the byssus opening and severely stress small clams. There are also worms and snails that drill holes through the clam shell. See *The Reef Aquarium*, Vol. One for detailed descriptions of these.*

The list includes, but is not limited to mantis shrimp, black spiny brittle starfish, and *Aiptasia* anemones.* Mantis shrimp can pop, pierce and munch giant clams, so beware of them and remove them by all means possible. The spiny black brittle star may reach into the siphons and irritate or injure the clam, so avoid including them. Keep the so called "serpent stars" instead. *Aiptasia* anemones are a problem with clams because they grow and multiply attached in the safety of the clams shell ridges, and when they expand they burn the clam's mantle wherever they touch it. Injecting the *Aiptasia*'s with hot freshwater or potassium hydroxide solution, among other possibilities, can take care of the problem. You might also brush the anemones off with a toothbrush in a bucket of seawater.

There are also parasites and diseases which affect clams. Two notable parasitic snails which are of concern are *Cymatium muricinum* and *Tathrella iredalei*. The former is not so common, and does not reproduce in the aquarium, but it can be introduced with live rock. It finds its way to the clam's mantle by crawling up through the byssal opening or it may simply reside between the mantle tissue and shell. If you suspect its presence, look for it with a flashlight, and if you can, remove the snail with a tweezers. If you are not sure you see a snail, don't go poking the clam with a tweezers which would cause injury. *Cymatium muricinum* grow to about the size of a dime, but it is the little ones you have to watch out for. *Tathrella iredalei* is a pyramidellid snail which looks something like a grain of white rice, more pointed on one end. They lay eggs and are very capable of reproducing in tremendous proportions in the aquarium. If they are present, you will see them on the edge of the shell just under the mantle, and around the byssus opening on the underside of the clam. They are easily removed with a tweezers, but difficult to eradicate once they've established themselves in an aquarium. They may be easier to spot on the clams at night using a flashlight.**

**The pyramidellid snails lay a gelatinous egg mass on the shell. This should be brushed off with a toothbrush to help control their population. Small wrasses including the Sixline Wrasse and Red Coris eat the snails and can help keep them in check.*

The only diseases I know which affect giant clams are bacterial infections. In fact I would venture to say that bacterial infection is the most common threat and cause

of death. This appears to be why the clams die so quickly. If I had the time and financial resources necessary, I
would investigate this further, but for now, suffice it to
say that a sick clam may benefit from antibiotic treatment
as if it were a fish. Good luck with your reef tank and
future pet clams, Elgie!

Q. Hello Julian
I'd like to open by saying how much I enjoy your column. Your's is cutting edge material and is the first thing
I turn to each month. I also appreciate the fact that
FAMA is truly hobbyist oriented, unlike the others I occasionally read which are decidedly industry oriented.
Here in the Ozarks, sources of information, hardware,
and livestock, particularly for the reef enthusiast, are few
and far between and *FAMA* plays an important role in
my participation in the hobby.

My question has to do with algal succession as an indica-
tor of water quality in the reef aquarium. As an organic
farmer, I have come to appreciate the fact that certain
misplaced plants ("weeds" to most folks) are valuable
indicators of soil conditions such as pH, soil texture,
drainage, mineral content, etc., and I've often wondered
if the same might hold true in regards to marine algae in
the reef tank.

I established a 29 gallon reef tank 12 months ago and I
have observed a clear and steady progression of "volun-
teer" macroalgae. (the only algae which I have introduced was a small portion of *Caulerpa prolifera*, which
proved to be quite unnecessary.) Within six weeks of
establishment, I began to notice a steady progression of
over 20 different types including, in more or less this
order, *C. prolifera, C. taxifolia, C. sertularioides,
Polyphysa polyphysoides, Acetabularia calyculus,
Batophora oerstedii, Valonia aegagrophila,
Dictyosphaeria cavernosa, Rosenvingea sanctae-crucis,
Champia parvula, Neomeris annulata, Halimeda dis-
coidea, Peyssonnelia* sp., *Hydrolithon boergesenii,
Gracilaria* sp., *Halimeda incrassata, Padina* sp., *C.
racemosa* var. *peltata*, and several unidentified species.
Several have come and gone (*Gracillaria, Padina,*

Rosenvingea, Dictyosphaeria, Neomeris, Polyphysa, and
Acetabularia) while new ones are still appearing. Is this
part of the normal life cycle of these algae or is it somehow related to environmental conditions?

You have often noted the response of "undesirables" to
elevated phosphate levels and I wonder if other algae
respond similarly to other variables such as potassium,
sulphate, carbonate, bicarbonate, pH, D.O., etc. If so,
and if these responses could be documented, this would
provide the aquarist with valuable insights into changing
water conditions. I'm not suggesting that such information would substitute for for tesating, but rather that it
could be another tool for the aquarist to assess the
health of the reef, particularly for those variables which
are difficult or expensive to test for.

The conditions in my tank are as follows:

pH: 8.3, ammonia, nitrite both 0, nitrate <1ppm.
Water changes 10% weekly with Reef Crystals,
Filtration by home-built trickle filter with 50,000 yds.
fishing line (recently replaced with 2 gal bioballs) and a
7x9 inch DLS roll, Chemi-Pure® and Polyfilter®.

Lighting is by two 40W HO Tritinics, two 20W Actinic
Days, one 20W GE WS.

My makeup water comes from a spring recently lab
tested as follows: Na 4ppm, Ca 72ppm, Mg 3ppm, Cl
2ppm, TDS 261, SAR 0.1, SO_4 11ppm, NO_3
.43ppm, pH 7.7, CO_3 0, HCO_3 180ppm, $CaCO_3$
190ppm, P .19ppm, K 1ppm, B < 0.1ppm.

If you have any insights, comments or thoughts on the
points I've brought up, I would be interested to hear
them. Thanks in advance and keep up the good work.
For the reefs,
Gordon Watkins,
Parthenon, AR

A. What you observed is both a result of the natural life
cycle of the algae and environmental conditions. When a

reef tank is first established there is excess food (nitrogen, phosphate) available owing to some rock fouling. This stimulates rapid plant growth and succession. Little is known about the complete requirements of marine algae, but certain elements are known to be important. Iodine is essential for the brown algae such as *Sargassum, Padina*, and *Dictyota*. Iron is important for most species, and is easily depleted. Your spring probably has a fair amount of iron, though it was not tested for. I noticed the results indicate a significant amount of Phosphate and Nitrate as well... watch out!* Your comments are interesting. I think that marine botanists would be interested in your notes on the disappearance and reappearance of certain species, as the life histories of algae, particularly of the red species, are poorly documented. Aquarists can provide valuable insights which are useful to researchers, assuming the researchers allow us to keep our aquaria, but I digress... You should read Charles Delbeek's article, "Live Rock Algal Succession In A Reef System," the very subject that interests you, Gordon, in the October 1990 issue of FAMA. By the looks of your algae identifying ability, I'd guess that you own a copy of *Marine Plants Of The Caribbean: A field Guide from Florida to Brazil* published by the Smithsonian Institution press. This is a very useful book as the color photographs make identification of many common species quite simple.

*When there is sufficient denitrification occurring in the rocks and sand, the input of nitrate from makeup water is harmless and does not lead to accumulation of nitrate.

Happy gardening!

I was just speaking to Seth Kolker, president of the Brooklyn Aquarium Society about one fishy topic or another, and he hoped I would announce that his club is having me over to speak on March 13, 1991. I will show slides of some very beautiful aquariums, give away a few "secrets," and of course, answer your questions. I pity the fool who can't make it there.

March 1992

Worms again!

Q. Dear Julian:
Over a period of 15 months that I have had my tank set up I have run across various types of small organisms

introduced with the live rock. There are two particular
types of worms that I'm concerned about, one type is a
hair thin almost elastic like white worm which seems to
stretch across rock to rock, only to retract quite rapidly
when disturbed. And the other is red, somewhat smaller
in length, but has the same hair thin elastic characteristics.

I questioned a number of people about this, from aquarium shop owners to hobbyists like myself, a few of them
have seen these worms in their tanks but all seem to have
a different opinion, that's when I decided to write you.

My questions to you are, with the description I gave you,
can you identify these worms? Are they tape worms?
Can they be harmful to any fish, plant or invertebrate in
a closed system like a reef tank? And my final question,
even though it's only common sense to insure proper
hygiene during tank maintenance, do you know of any
case and is it possible either through accidental ingestion
of water during siphoning, or through a hand wound,
etc. for these worms to be transmitted to humans?
Brian Spadaccia, Yorktown heights, NY

A. Brian, transmittal of the common "reef tapeworm"
may even be accomplished when the human host merely
watches the aquarium. Symptoms of the affliction
include INSATIABLE APPETITE for any and all products
that have the words "reef" or "bio--" contained in the
name, total dissatisfaction with one's aquarium despite
the praise of fellow hobbyists and, ultimately, insanity
once the worm works it's way up into the brain. There is
no cure.

But seriously, folks, the worms Brian described are not
really worms at all, but are the FEEDING TENTACLES of a
type of worm called terebellid or spaghetti worm, which I
have described in this column at least twice before. Worm
questions are very common, in fact, and it seems I get at
least one about the terebellid variety whenever I give a
lecture somewhere. Terebellid worms are harmless. The
worm lives in the rocks and puts out its long feeding tentacles to gather detritus particles from the surrounding
rocks and bottom. It ingests the detritus to eat the bacteria

and other microorganisms living thereon.

It is possible to become infected with parasitic worms by INGESTING fish or some invertebrates with the parasites, but this is a danger reserved for the do-it-yourself people who prepare sushi at home. I don't know of any incidence of parasitism from mere handling or contact with invertebrates in a saltwater aquarium.

The only thing I should caution you about regards nematocysts and bacteria. Corals and anemones can really give people a serious sting with their nematocysts, and the fact that their mucous is fertile ground for bacteria creates a potentially risky situation for the hobbyist who gets stung on an open wound. The nematocyts and their poison causes destruction of tissue which generally manifests itself immediately as localized pain. This wouldn't be so bad except that the bacteria may take the opportunity to make camp and create a lovely white topped red mountain of an infection... which is a potentially life threatening situation and that is no joke. If you discover that after handling a coral, anemone, or live rock that you have developed a rash or a painful reddened sore, you may need to see a physician. Usually a rash or sore spot that arises after handling live rock is caused by roughing the skin, which is not suprisingly a common malady for bricklayers, but it may also be caused by tiny glass fibers from sponges or bristle worms, producing a rash very much like you've been mishandling fiberglass. The larger bristle worms may inject a poison with their bristles, producing a painful sting very much like the sting of a poisonous caterpillar. These irritations go away on their own and are soothed with creams containing cortisone, but an infection may not go away on its own, and may continue to destroy healthy tissue. A physician can determine whether the infection requires the administration of antibiotics. If you have cut yourself while working in your tank, it is a good idea to apply Neosporin ointment and a bandaid to the wound after thoroughly rinsing it with running water to remove any foreign particles. This is a precaution to prevent an infection, but if you think you have an infection originating from your aquarium SEE A DOCTOR ok?

Q. Dear Julian,

I am currently using a Sandpoint R.O. system to filter water into plastic trash cans for use in my reef tank. I would like to know if there are rules regarding water storage? i.e. can water be stored indefinitely? If the water is not aerated can it produce toxins? There is a slime that forms on the plastic (bacteria?). Can this be a problem? My many books don't really mention anything about longer term storage of water, so anything you can tell me would be of help. Thanks, Bill McGinnis, Annandale, MN

A. How refreshing, a question about water. Yes, water can be stored indefinitely, but there are some important aspects of storage you should know, and I'm glad you brought up the question. You are using reverse osmosis to filter your water. This process produces very pure water. Assuming you shelled out the dough and went to the trouble to install such a unit because you wanted pure water, it stands to reason that you want to prevent this water from going bad or losing purity. Well, pure water is a really good solvent...you can imagine the purified water being like a sponge in that it will soak up impurities from the air. Two things can be deduced from this property of the water. You should store it in a closed/covered vessel, and you should not aerate it. Of course the vessel you store it in should be inert. Regarding the slime coat you noticed, yes that's bacteria. While these are not really a problem, you may hinder their growth by employing ozonation or U.V. sterilization.

A further aspect of this question might include the storage of saltwater. Basically, you may store saltwater in a closed, inert container as long as you wish. There is no need to aerate or stir it, though it doesn't hurt to do so. It will pick up oxygen and equilibrate with the atmosphere when you pour it out.

Q. Dear Julian,

I have recently sent a letter to Mr. B. Michael Mclemore stating my position on the subject of banning collection of marine tropicals. I, like yourself, am a biologist and an aquarium keeper. In addition, I am also an environmentalist in the manner of co-existence with the environment instead of pillaging it. I agree that many environmental organizations spout off their mouths before all of the facts are clear or with no scientific backup at all. What would be very nice to see would be acceptable quotas placed on collectors in assigned collection areas. These quotas should be based on hard scientific data concerning reproduction rates for affected fish populations and time needed for growth to marketable size. In addition, I believe that fish species that do not survive well in captivity should not be harvested until more research has been done into their manner of life so that keeping them in captivity would be more successful.

In addition, I would like to state why I believe that aquarists are an easy target for legislation. While being a president of an aquarium society for some time, I came to realize that the majority of aquarium keepers are quiet people who normally do not speak out. The people that speak out and write articles for magazines such as this one are in the minority in this hobby. It takes a major act to excite them to a high enough level to take up a pen and state their viewpoints. I do hope that your warning and the impending legislation will be enough of a major act.

In closing, Julian, I would recommend that we as a hobby should do what we can to stop irresponsible and alarmist attitudes from dictating what or whatnot is allowed as pets. But, on the flip-side, we must get better about policing our own. It is kind of hard to defend our point in recent light of what has been happening in the Philippines since the marine trade started.
Sincerely,
Terry F. Fairfield,
Loves Park, IL.

A. Thanks for the comments, Terry. Your quota idea is sort of employed in Florida through the use of trip tickets and daily boat/bag limits for collectors. Certain size limits have also been legislated in for many targetted species. Size limits protect the breeding stock and prevent the premature capture of "tinies" which have low survival in the handling process. I concur with you on the issue of species known to have poor survival in captivity, and I would also extend such restriction to species known to grow too large for the average aquarium... our public aquariums can only take so many groupers and sharks off our hands. I would not suggest a ban on the import of any of the fish which fall into these categories, as this would require additional customs inspections, rather I think the industry could employ a system of supply and demand with these fish whereby the pet dealer may specifically order these species when a customer requests them. In this manner the end buyer is most likely to be prepared to care for the animal. Life certainly is not so simple, and changing old habits is very difficult, but perhaps it is possible for us to restrict the availability of problem species.

I wanted to add to your comments about hobbyists being an easy target. Marinelife fisherman were also a target I refered to in my column, and they are an easy target because they are relatively poor. Big money makes policy much more easily than common sense and fairness to the individual or the environment. With only rare exceptions, if you have enough money, you can dredge a boat channel, renourish a beach, clear trees to build a road, or bury marine habitat to expand a road. The fact that these practices result in a decline in the health of the environment produces an urgent need to find a scapegoat for the observed decline. When policy restricts the activities of the marinelife fisherman, the state can pat itself on the back about the terrific job it is doing at saving the environment. Remember, to keep our lovely big hotels from falling into the sea it's O.K. to smother miles of coral reef with dredge sediment, killing so many species, including coral, but you musn't remove a single living polyp because there is ZERO TOLERANCE for that.

Back to the subject of fishes that don't fare well in captivity, I don't know how we can begin to limit their collection and importation, since it is not the simple matter of the wholesale facilities not ordering them... they just take what's sent mostly. Declaring a boycott never works because too many hobbyists don't read, aren't aware, or are new to the hobby... how many of you reading this now recall Steve Robinson's articles on the Philippines? I

*With the present rate of success in growing small polyped stony corals such as *Acropora* and *Porites* species, it is now possible to maintain coral polyp feeding fishes in a large aquarium (several thousand gallons) full of growing coral. I have seen successful care even in much smaller aquariums with the orangespotted filefish, *Oxymonoacanthus longirostris*, which feeds on *Acropora* polyps primarily but also on other coral polyps, zoanthids, and crustaceans. I have seen that when kept in an aquarium with sufficient small polyped corals to graze they do little harm to the coral and can even learn to take prepared foods.

As of this writing the AZA and the Marine Aquarium Society of North America are working on species lists and a system for educating dealers and buyers about potentially difficult species. Dealer and importer certification programs are also planned.

suppose that if a group of hobbyists, ie a club, got together and published a list of fish (with photographs) that they feel should not be collected except when specially ordered, and this published list were provided in quantities to the major fish distributors who could send copies to their suppliers, who could likewise supply their collectors with the same published work (the photos bridge the language barrier), then maybe it might work... but I'm not certain... people resist change. Why should they stop sending the fish when people keep buying them? I'd like to take this opportunity to list fishes that I think should be available only on request... I encourage commentary on this.

Chaetodon trifasciatus - a
C. triangulum - a
C. larvatus - a
C. ornatissimus - a
C. melapterus - a
Zanclus cornutus - b
Philippine Regal angel - d
Hawaiian Cleaner Wrasse - e
Canary Blenny - d

C. trifascialis - a
C. baronessa - a
C. myeri - a
C. austriacus - a
C. reticulatus - a
orangespotted filefish - d
Multifasciatus Angel - b,d
Pinnatus Batfish - b
Certain groupers, sharks - c

Key:
a = eats coral polyps only.
b = requires special care in handling, aquarium planning, and diet. Can be hardy, but most specimens do not survive long.
c = grows too large for most home aquaria.
d = has special dietary requirements or suffers from collection with cyanide. Usually starves.
e = special dietary requirement. Eats parasites and dead tissue...usually starves unless kept in a large tank with many fish.

I am not the first to suggest that the term "assorted butterfly" be brought out of use, the problem with it being that it allows the importation of the assorted species listed above which do not survive. The term refers to a mix of butterflyfish species, some which do survive well and some which don't, but more specifically they are all small juveniles. Here lies another point. Even the "assort-ed butterfly" species which are hardy are sometimes too small to survive the handling process because they have a high metabolism and food requirement. I think there should be a minimum size limit on imported butterfly-fishes, but again this could not be law because it would be difficult to enforce... it would have to be achieved through change in the system, which is unlikely.

We started with worms in this month's column, and per-haps I have re-opened the can by addressing this subject at such length. I would like to hear commentary from hobbyists and industry people about how self regulation might be possible. Perhaps we may be able to make a change.

I wanted to update you on the present situation regarding live rock collection in Florida. First, regarding Project Reefkeepers petition for emergency rulemaking on live rock, the Department of Commerce has rejected the peti-tion. However the State of Florida has taken steps of its own to ban live rock collection altogether from its adja-cent (federal) waters. You should recall that live rock col-lection from Florida state waters was banned in 1989, while collection from federal waters has continued since then. While Florida can't directly ban the collection of rock in federal waters, what it plans to do is to ban land-ings of the rock, which basically achieves the same end as a ban on collection. This ban on landings has been discussed for some time now, with an emphasis on a transition to aquaculture being offered as a solution to the loss of income and product that the ban would effect. Initially it was suggested that the ban on landings would be put into effect two years after the rule was made, with the rationale that it would take this long to establish viable aquaculture ventures. Of course the environmen-talists feel this is too long of a delay, and the marinelife fisherman feel it isn't enough time, considering that get-ting started will take at least a year, and the growth time needed for marketable rock is unkown. At the latest hear-ing, it appeared that the rule would allow the harvest of live rock for three more years, with reductions in land-ings over the period. It will be interesting to see how such reductions will be enforced. I think aquaculture is an exciting alternative to collection, and I look forward to the day when a reef tank may be set up with live rock, corals, and other marinelife all raised in captivity. If the state of Florida is serious about aquaculture of live rock as an alternative to harvest, then it has a lot of work to do to make the task of getting started possible. Imagine how frustrating it might be for the marinelife fisherman who, after having the source of his livelihood taken away on the basis of emotional speculation, meets all sorts of obstacles, delays, and barriers which prevent him from achieving an aquaculture business which the state promised as a solution. This issue was addressed at the latest hearing, and fortunately there was a move to begin having workshops on aquaculture immediately, probably the most hopeful outcome of the entire hearing.

One might wonder if the ban on landings of live rock will affect the importation of rock and invertebrates from overseas. Not to worry for now, at least, as the state does not have jurisdiction over that matter. Still, the CITES meeting in Japan this spring may offer some new obstacles for the reef keeping hobby, depending on whether the federal government makes any changes in policy based on decisions made by CITES.*

*No changes occurred.

My position has always been that live rock is a renewable resource, and that removal of loose rock from the extensive, heavily disturbed rubble zones created by storms does not pose any threat to the reef or environment as a whole. Unfortunately there is too much emotionally charged opposition based on erroneous notions about live rock and its removal, and blatantly false claims about significant impact to the environment. I am concerned that the ban in Florida, not to mention the ban also presently in effect in Hawaii, sets a precedent that we reef keeping hobbyist are involved in a morally deplorable practice of habitat destruction. We must make it clear that such is not the case, and that our hobby affords a unique opportunity for education, and increases the public awareness of reef ecology. Still, there is room for self regulation in the marine aquarium hobby, particularly with regard to fish collecting and handling practices, and fishes which shouldn't even be caught in the first place. By the way, I goofed in telling you to send comments to B. Michael McLemore, and I gave you the wrong suite # in the adress, which should have read #116, not #118 as I wrote... honestly it looks like 118 on the fax transmission I recieved from Paul Loiselle. Your letters were recieved, not to worry (and thank you), though in the future you might send comments about live rock to Dr. William W. Fox, Jr., Assistant Administrator for Fisheries, NOAA, NMFS, Silver Spring Metro Center #1. 1335 East-West Highway, Silver Spring, MD. 20910. There is really nothing you can do about the state ruling now as the decisions have already been made, but I think that making your voice and opinion known on a national level could raise government awareness of the importance of our hobby, so don't hesitate to inform them about the success you are having with your reef aquariums, the value that Florida live rock had in making that success happen, and your concern about those practices which really have a detrimental impact on the coastal environment, especially in Florida, such as dredging, beach renourishment, and pollution.

April 1992

Q. Dear Julian
I have a couple of problems with my marine fish tank- hope you can help me out. The background specifics:

Mechanics
-28 gallon plexiglass hex
-external hanging box filter (Aquaclear 200)
-Undergravel filter driven by powerhead (Aquaclear 201)
-Reverse flow protein skimmer (Aquarium technologies) driven by Elite 802
-Bubble wand driven by Optimal (German) @ 250L/hr.
-two 15" lightbulbs (Spectrum V, 14watts each)
-3" of crushed coral (Mexican) substrate
-tank is next to patio (sliding glass) door, facing west, and recieves only indirect sunlight due to translucent patio roof, but I placed a blue translucent film on that side of tank to filter out the red end of the spectrum - initially had lots of green algae, but now have a little mixed green, brown, and black algae.

Chemistry
-Temp =78 degrees F
-pH   =8.3
-dKH   =14.0 to 7.0 German (first problem)
-S.G.   =1.022
-NH_3 =zero
-NO_2 =zero
-NO_3 =<10ppm

Population
-1 Blue Damsel
-1 Banded Gobie
-2 species of *Caulerpa*
-1 strange, unidentified creature (other problem)

Maintenance
-I do a 25% water change once a month using "cured" natural ocean water. (cured + 4 weeks in a sealed container in the dark followed by pH and S.G. balancing and 24 hours aeration).
-Bi-monthly doses of vitamins and trace elements per package directions.
-Food is rotated: flake, Formula One frozen, and live brine shrimp. Fish are fed once every day.

History
I seeded the tank with gravel from a local aquarium shop and broke the tank in with the damselfish - (Note: it had a bacterial infection which appeared shortly after it first arrived - cured that in two weeks with antibiotics in a hospital tank and it's doing well now four months later).

My intent is to trade the damsel back and have a tank with very gentle creatures; seahorses, another goby, and a cow fish or two (Camel cows are my favorite).

Problems
1st problem: I can't seem to keep the degrees of carbonate hardness up at 15 to 18 level. I have been adding Marine Buffer constantly. The fellows at the aquarium shop said it was because of the new crushed coral substrate and that it would eventually stabilize, but they couldn't say how long that would take... Why is the dKH

Photo by Jules Resnick

dropping a degree or two every few days and how can I stabilize it at the appropriate level?

2nd problem: A flatworm (?) apparently came into the tank with the seed gravel from the aquarium shop. He has grown rapidly from less than 1/4" long when first seen to about an inch long now. He is completely black except for the bottom of his "foot" which is banana yellow. He has a thin, rippled fringe all around his perimeter with his "feelers" emerging from underneath this. He appears to have a slit along the center of his back - also covered by this rippled fringe. Occasionally I can see in this slit some light grey color (could it be the start of the formation of a shell?) He is doing fine in the big tank - apparently grazing at night on algae and food which the fish miss (I did see him make his way to a piece of "Formula One" food which the damsel missed leading me to believe he is omnivorous, rather than merely herbivorous). He hides during the day so I assume he is nocturnal. Moe's book says that there are 15,000 species of flatworms, some of which are parasitic to vertebrates. This is what worries me, so I want to identify this animal. Enclosed is a picture taken by my friend and associate, Jules Resnick from which I hope you will be able to make an ID. (I would greatly appreciate it if you would convince your publisher to publish this picture in your magazine and give Jules the appropriate credit as he spent alot of time and effort to get just the right picture - thanks!)

Though I know it may be difficult, can you please identify this creature and, if it is a flatworm, tell which flatworm this is and whether or not I have to worry about him (or about parasitism) with the planned fish population?

I would greatly appreciate any help/advice you can give. Sincerely yours, Christopher Bekins, Menlo Park, CA

A. Your second problem is neither a problem nor a flatworm. The flatworms which are harmful to vertebrates are generally small... on the order of a quarter inch or less. There are flatworms which are much larger, but they are really flat. They do not sport the double decker design like your black beast with the foot and separate rippled fringe mantle, though the outer edge of a flatworm may ripple as it glides over the substrate. What you have in your tank isn't a flatworm, but a mollusk called a limpet, whose primary diet is algae, though they will occasionally nibble on other food as you noted. Consider yourself lucky to have such a pet! I have noted that a Caribbean species which looks like yours, but in which the mantle is entirely yellow-orange instead of black, is a good algae eater and scavenger in fish tanks, but in a reef tank it can occasionally nibble on both soft coral and stony coral tissue, so I avoid it with live corals. I think I discussed flatworms before, when a hobbyist asked about the harmless types which appear to eat diatoms. These may proliferate explosively in an aquarium with strong illumination and diatom growth stimulated by excess silicates in the water. They are harmless. However, there are similar appearing flatworms which are harmful to corals and anemones.* There are also flatworms which do no harm to the corals, anemones, or plants which they live on, but are really unsightly when they proliferate in the aquarium. My deepest sympathy to those of you who have the plague of planaria in your reef tank. Most typically these can bee seen as 1/8" round, flat disks creeping along the surface of mushroom anemones, leather corals, or even the tentacles of stony corals. Generally they are brownish, but they may blend with the color of their host. No-one has found the natural predator for these pests, as far as I know. When I was diving off the Whitsunday Islands in Australia, I

*These flatworms are probably only commensals, but they do irritate the corals when they are abundant, and they can shade the coral's tissue.

found an area about the size of half an acre covered by *Sarcophyton* leather corals which were all closed up and "freckled" by a parasitic flatworm. My observation confirms that they may proliferate unchecked even in the wild. It is possible either that natural salinity fluctuations as occur during the rainy season for reefs near the Australian coast, or seasonal temperature swings are the natural control for the planaria. Still, it seems that there should be something which eats them.

Peter Wilkens recommends a freshwater dip (about a minute or two in duration) to make the worms drop off the affected coral or anemone. In time this procedure, using the specimen as "bait" could eliminate the problem. This procedure could also be used to prevent introduction of the worms in the first place. One might also try a drop in salinity to rid an aquarium of this problem, but I caution you that this must be done with care. If your tank has planaria coating everything, siphoning them off can help reduce the population to a point where they may be eliminated with freshwater dips or a salinity drop. Unfortunately there are no better recommendations.

Your first problem is not a problem at all either, Chris. It is an artifact of misleading information. If you stop adding the buffer, you will find that your dKH will fall to about seven or eight, which is just right... at least that's what it is in the ocean. It might hover a little above this, say maybe ten or twelve*, which is fine, but you do not need to add the buffer unless the dKH falls below seven. I am concerned by your described "pH balancing" of the natural ocean water. It should not need to be buffered... have you checked the pH after aerating the water?

In retrospect it seems you don't have any problems with your tank at all... just concerns and that's ok. I have two concerns to pass on to you in the hopes of preventing future real problems. First, your affection for cowfish is understandable as they do have a sparkling charm, not to mention a bizarre figure, but I want to caution you that despite their hardiness, they are very prone to chronic "Ich" infestation, both *Cryptocaryon* and Oodinium. You must

*Calcification can be enhanced by maintaining a carbonate hardness slightly above natural seawater values. Some aquarists consider a dKH of 10 ideal. The alkalinity can be a source of carbon instead of the depleted CO_2 typical during the daytime in closed system aquariums with high rates of photosynthesis.

*There is a frozen Mysis shrimp from Idaho available now from a company called Piscine Enegetics. This food is readily eaten by seahorses and apparently supplies all their nutritional needs. Please see an article by Jeff Campsen and George Paleudis about successful culture of seahorses in the Summer 1995 issue of Aquarium Frontiers.

quarantine them with copper treatment for a couple of weeks before introducing them to your display tank. Judging by your experience with the damsel, it sounds like you are prepared to treat the fish separately... that's good. If you plan to succeed in keeping seahorses, I just wanted to be sure that you didn't plan on feeding just brine shrimp. While seahorses will enthusiastically slurp them down, the brine shrimp don't meet all the nutritional requirements, resulting in a much shortened life span. You should feed one or more of the following food items to be sure the horses are getting complete nutrition: grass or "glass" shrimp, *Gammarus* (amphipods), and live baby guppies or mollies. You can also train the seahorses to eat right out of your hand, if you are patient. Training them will allow you to feed frozen foods, though you should offer live food occasionally as it is also important for their nutrition. I don't know where in California Menlo Park is, but if you live near the coast, you can collect all sorts of tasty (to seahorses) little crustaceans and fish in tidepools filled with algae.*

Q. Dear Mr. Sprung,
I've never kept a marine tank before, but the other day I saw a product (Magic Ocean) which claims I can keep marine fish and freshwater fish in the aquarium simultaneously. They talk about "osmotic Pressure" in fish skin, and suggest a specific gravity of 1.008.
My questions are simple. First, is this stuff for real? And second, would the idea work with any good quality marine salt at the same specific gravity?
Of course this could open some new doors regarding species compatibility. What do you think a damselfish would make of a Central American Cichlid? Any advice that you would offer will be greatly appreciated.
Sincerely, Walt Perkins, Edwards, CA.

A. Yes, Walt, it's for real, though I would hardly call it magic, and I personally don't think the idea of mixing the hobbies is so progressive, though as a scientist I am always curious about ideas which stretch the limits of physiological laws, because there's always room for discovery.

The idea of mixing fresh and saltwater fishes in the same tank is contrary to the goal of providing a natural environment for the species being maintained, and this unnatural element of the product you mention disturbs me. But of course one does not have to use such a product solely for the purpose of having goldfish and tangs munching duckweed side by side.

I recall seeing such a product many years ago and haven't seen it advertised for quite some time. I don't know if there is a comeback imminent, or if you merely ran across some old stock. I never experimented with it so I can't really comment on the validity of the claims. I can tell you that I have seen healthy communities of tropical marinelife along Florida's west coast where freshwater springs meet the ocean, and the specific gravity is often about 1.010 or less. In my coursework in school I learned that a high calcium level in the water was the reason for the success of these communities. Perhaps that is part of the secret to this magic salt.

One interesting aspect of maintaining fishes in such brackish water is the possibility of reducing incidence of disease. I recall hearing about experiments done at the Shedd Aquarium with low salinity, and many hobbyists have told me about their own successful experiments with marine fish. I have no experience or correspondence regarding freshwater species and longterm maintenance in brackish water.

Q. Dear Mr. Dewey,
I am writing to you, first to commend you on your efforts with the FAMA magazine and second to get some information on how to proceed in contacting people in the industry that are involved with the research end of marine and reef aquarium keeping. I have been keeping a reef tank for the last 21 months and have come to realize this is something I would like to do as a life's work. I am particularly interested in the research of possible captive coral reproduction and the many symbiotic relationships in the ocean we do not see in our aquariums. Any information you can provide me will be greatly appreciated. Thank you for your time.
Sincerely, Anthony Velasco, Lawrenceville, GA
P.S. Maybe Mr. Sprung can drop me a line too.

A. Maybe Mr. Sprung will. At least I'll discuss your question here. Your question is superficially such a simple one, but to answer it I find there are many subtleties I'd like to address and, frankly I'm glad you asked.

That you should want to make aquarium related research your life's work is understandable and admirable, but your own talents, determination, and planning are key to making such a career move a wise decision. To do it in such a way that you are financially secure is no simple task. Personally I think for most people it is not a wise move to make aquarium research more than just a hobby, but for those who wish to do so, more power to you! If you plan to start by opening up a fish shop or starting an aquarium maintenance business, you may find that your love of aquariums and research will be squashed by the need to earn a buck, and you may never find the time to do what you really want to do. Working for public aquaria may fulfill your dreams, but most often there will not be the time or money there for your research (though this is not always the case, especially if you are very motivated and able to secure grant funding). You will have to put in a lot of time before you will earn a decent salary. The same is true for doing aquarium research as a biologist. For some reason our society admires the valuable work of biologists, but does not reward them financially for their work, as it does for other professionals, like lawyers, for instance. Your own ingenuity, not credentials, will determine your worth to society if you wish to pursue a career as a biologist.

Do not misunderstand my points about these different aspects of the aquarium field. There is no direct path to success, and the more experience you have with all types of work in aquariums, the greater the chance you will succeed in your goal.

In the aquarium industry there is tremendous room for research, but there isn't tremendous funding available for it. Most of the aquarium industry manufacturers are small companies. They do some research, but this is really nothing compared to the research done by enthusiastic hobbyists. It has been my experience that the most progressive, important, and original research is performed by hobbyists in their homes.

On this subject, I recently had a long and enlightening talk with Mark Derr, who was interviewing me for an article he was writing for Audubon magazine which should be appearing in the spring, at about the same time as this column. The article concerns the aquarium hobby and specifically addresses issues such as live rock and coral harvesting. One aspect of our conversation which I found very frustrating because I didn't feel that he understood my point concerned the subject of research by hobbyists. I have publicly stated my belief that hobbyists' research is as valuable as or more valuable than any research being done by scientists on aquariums. Mr. Derr questioned my assertion, specifically asking me why scientists were not aware of the fabulous work being done by hobbyists, why hobbyists didn't publish their findings in reputable scientific journals. For example, he told me it is not generally accepted by the scientific community that stony corals can be grown and propagated long term in closed system aquaria, even though hobbyists have documented success in the aquarium literature. Naturally I took offense to the idea that hobbyists have a duty to report to the scientific community. On the contrary, I feel that the scientific community concerned with coral reefs has a duty to keep up with aquarium literature which is every bit as valid as their own literature. I explained to Mr. Derr that for most people aquarium keeping and reef keeping was a HOBBY, not work. For the scientist it is part of the JOB to report discoveries... hobbyists cannot be expected to write papers on their experience, but when they do, those scientists who could benefit by the information should make sure they subscribe to the journals or belong to the clubs whose publications contain information of value to them.

Now aside from getting that off my chest there really is a point to bringing our conversation up. Until recently, most hobbyists (never mind scientists) were unaware of what hobbyists in other states were doing, and in other countries? you might as well be talking about other planets! This is changing now, with the formation of larger "parent" organizations of hobbyists, and through the efforts of aquarium journals. These organizations have also been pursuing conservation issues and the prospect of regulating the aquarium industry. I refer specifically to Ocean Voice International, the International Marinelife Alliance, The Marine Aquarium Society of North America, and the International Marine Aquarist Association. If you wish to keep up with research pertaining to coral reefs and aquariums, I encourage you to join these groups. Although all the gaps are not yet bridged between aquarium societies in different countries, and there is yet much useful information to share, I believe in time a sort of "new world order" will establish firm ties between aquarium societies worldwide.*

Another organization you should join, Anthony, is the American Association of Zoological Parks and Aquariums(AAZPA). Their newsletter keeps you informed on research being done at zoos and aquariums, and even lists opportunities you may wish to pursue.**

I don't know how to bridge the gap between the scientific community and the hobby of aquarium keeping. Public aquariums have sort of bridged this gap, but there is also a gap between the hobbyist level and the public aquariums. I know a lot of hobbyists keep up with the scientific literature, and use the information they find to improve their technique. Somehow there needs to be an acceptance that what hobbyists are doing is valuable...that's all, but how to gain that acceptance?

A few months ago I made a reference to aquariums in Holland, stating that there was a preference there for heavily planted marine algae aquariums, as we first a saw in the articles which George Smit wrote that appeared in FAMA in 1986. Well, I should not have made such a general statement about Dutch reef tanks, for while they still practice the heavily planted freshwater gardens, the *Caulerpa* covered reef tanks are no longer so common, as was observed by Charles Delbeek in his recent trip there. Charles has prepared an article about his trip for *Aquarium Fish Magazine*. You will have to

---

*Internet, Compuserve, and the world wide web have dramatically assisted in this regard.

**The International Society for Reef Studies (ISRS) is another organization of interest to reef keeping aquarists. They publish the Journal *Coral Reefs*. Membership for the ISRS is $60.00/yr currently, which includes the journal *Coral Reefs* and the newsletter *Reef Encounter*. With these two publications you will learn about the latest research on coral reef biology and geology, reef corals, and associated marinelife. You will also be informed about current events from around the world pertaining to coral reefs and coral reef related symposia, new publications, computer databases, as well as legislation affecting reefs and our hobby worldwide. There is also a tremendous opportunity for aquarists to correspond or network with contributing editors and researchers. An annual directory lists members with their current

address, phone # and
E-mail address. For
membership contact:
Daphne G. Fautin,
Ph.D., Treasurer, ISRS
Kansas Geological
Survey Campus West
1930 Constant Ave.
University of Kansas
Lawrence, KS 66045
USA

wait for it to get all the details...no "leaks" here.

For your reference:
AAZPA
Oglebay Park
Wheeling, WV 26003
(304) 242-2160

Ocean Voice International
2883 Otterson Drive
Ottawa, Ontario K1V 7B2 Canada
(613) 990-8819; FAX (613) 521-4205

International Marinelife Alliance U.S.
94 Station Street, Suite 645
Hingham, MA 02043, U.S.A.
(617) 383-9915; FAX (617) 383-0081

International Marine Aquarist Association
P.O. Box 7
Ilminster, Somerset, TA19 9BY England
FAX 458-253081

Marine Aquarium Society of North America
P.O. Box 191261
Mobile, AL 36619

May 1992

Q. Dear Don,
Congratulations on closing another year and for making
FAMA better every time! I'm looking forward to 1992 issues
(and also my Pier to Peer article). After many years of fishkeeping, the last 3 of which have been strictly saltwater, I
believe I have an idea for a series of articles that will greatly
interest aquarists as well as unlock many mysteries they all
live with. Why not start a series called "What Was That?" or
"Did You See That?" Most aquarium books and magazines
show photos of (and discuss) the most common and frequently encountered organisms. "Rare and Unusual
Marines" strictly covers fish (I think), but no one ever shows
photos of or discusses the "unidentifiables" we occasionally
encounter. This type of article and photos would grab everyone's attention and covers a topic nowhere else seen.

Interest in these mysterious creatures (fish, inverts, plants, etc.) would generate reader participation (send *FAMA* photos of those bizarre creatures you can't identify) and *FAMA* would research them and discuss their name, growth potential, feeding, spawning, and whether they are a beneficial or dangerous inhabitant.

This topic is near and dear to me since I recently lost several healthy and costly fish in my reef tank to a mantis shrimp. I had no idea what it was and how dangerous and quick growing until I researched for several hours in several books in my library. I was fortunate enough to siphon him out in a few short minutes by luring him into a siphon tube with krill in it. I also discovered that it more than likely came from my live rock 1 year ago and probably grew from 1/2" to 4" in the year it was living in my tank. Once large enough its appetite grew to include my prized fish.

I've enclosed photos of my second and third mysterious finds respectively. The green "golf ball" is, I believe an algae bubble. Is it macro or micro? Where does it come from? Harmful or beneficial? Does the appearance and growth of them show good or poor conditions? Should they pop, is their liquid content harmful?

My true mystery is the photo of the orange (nudibranch?) I've enclosed. It's underbody is snail like with a head like a snail with antennae, and its upper body is covered with the same orange colored flesh about the size of a quarter and one-half as thin... well... "What Was That?" I anxiously await your thoughts and comments. Sincerely, Joseph DeMarte, 37 Winslow Road, White Plains, NY 10606

A. Well Joe, as you can see, Don forwarded your letter to me. I don't know whether the column you are suggesting will materialize, but such photos are likely to be sent to me or another contributing editor for comment. First I'd like to point out that a column of the scope you have suggested does exist in another publication called *Sea Frontiers*, published by the International Oceanographic Foundation in association with the

Ventricaria ventricosa, the bubble alga.

University of Miami. The monthly column is called "Sea Secrets". You may find subscription info by writing to Sea Frontiers,
P.O. Box 498, Mount Morris, IL 61054.

I guess we can add your baited siphon method to the list of ways to remove mantis shrimps. Luck plays a role in all the methods known so far.

The "algae bubble" is a green alga which used to be called *Valonia ventricosa* , but is now known as *Ventricaria ventricosa.* It is a time bomb. These otherwise beautiful plants which look like green sapphires under bright light are definitely not desirable guests in the aquarium, since they can multiply in explosive profusion and cover every surface of the rocks. They are dangerous to stony corals because they attach to them and as they grow and spread they push back the living coral tissue away from the skeleton. Don't get hung up on categorizing algae into the two groups, "macro" and "micro," as this information is misleading. (ie. people tend to generalize the notion of microalgae as "bad-guy" and macroalgae as "good-guy," when those distinctions are not necessarily true.)

Ventricaria is introduced into the aquarium with live rock or attached to pieces of live coral. Their appearance and subsequent growth is not an indication of water quality... they will grow profusely under all conditions. The fluid released when one of these bubbles pops is not harmful, but the result of popping them and allowing the fluid to leak out is the spread of the plague of bubble algae. The fluid contains spores which develop into new plants wherever the settle and they settle everywhere. Left alone to grow, a single bubble will swell up to an inch or more in size until one day when it becomes clear, and the green cytoplasm groups into blotches which become tiny new bubble algae that brood inside the original sac. The original bubble loses its pressure, deflates and decomposes, releasing the brood. Individual bubbles also multiply into clusters of bubbles which, when removed, apparently leave spores behind because new clusters soon reappear. The plague can be maddening. I do not know of a good herbivore to control them, though I'm sure that sea urchins would eat small ones. The best way to get rid of them is to siphon them off, or remove the rock and pick them off.*

*For additional tips about controlling bubble algae see volume one of this series and in *The Reef Aquarium* Vol. One. Large tangs, particularly *Zebrasoma* spp. do eat bubble algae, but they cannot be housed in small reef aquariums.

There are other, similar species such as *Valonia macrophysa*, which has more elongated bubbles that adhere very tightly to the substrate.

Your mystery nudibranch is not a nudibranch but a limpet. If some of you are having a deja-vou experience, don't worry, you have read this before... last month when a reader described a black limpet, and I mentioned the orange one. Well the pictures of this orange one were not suitable for print, but suffice it to say that this limpet is identical to the one featured last month except for the color. It is mostly a herbivore, but will feed on soft corals and stony corals on occasion... so I recommend that you remove it. I apologize that I don't know the name off the top of my head, but I know that it is a described species, and that I have seen it in a couple of old texts on Caribbean invertebrates. They are occasional under rocks at the low tide mark in Biscayne Bay around the man-made residential islands of Miami Beach, which means they are likely to be common in the Florida Keys in the same kind of habitat.

Q. Dear Julian,
In response to a reader's question in the February issue,
you mentioned that the addition of an oxygenator can produce "a very high supersaturation level of dissolved oxygen, which is toxic to many invertebrates." Could this situation also occur from the addition of a protein skimmer
and what types of invertebrates are likely to be affected?
I am also concerned about lighting. Right now I have
two strip lights, one with an Actinic bulb and the other a
Triton. Since I discovered *FAMA* only a few months ago,
I've begun to feel like the only person interested in
maintaining a reef tank who is not running a metal
halide or VHO system. Like many people these days
though, I haven't got an endless budget and simply can't
afford to spend $500 on a lighting system. However I do
want to be successful, so my question to you is: Is there
a quality alternative to these high priced systems which
will allow me to be successful at reef keeping?

A. Regarding the first question, no, a protein skimmer
causes no such difficulty. Very high supersaturation of
oxygen can achieve a toxic level only when pure oxygen
is administered to the aquarium under pressure. Air contains only about 20% oxygen at atmospheric pressure.

Regarding your second question about lighting, the
answer is yes, but you will have to match the lighting
with a suitable, SHALLOW aquarium. Inexpensive means
not especially bright, so you don't want the tank to be
too deep. If this is the way you want to do it, as a general guide I would recommend at least four full-tank-
length fluorescent bulbs per foot of tank width. If you
use the polished aluminum reflectors now available, or if
you choose bulbs with reflectors built-in, then you will
achieve intensity like H.O. tubes without reflectors. You
may also use a canopy as your reflector, though this is
not nearly as efficient as the aluminum reflectors. I suggest you try two blue tubes and two daylight type tubes,
if you are using only four bulbs. If you can afford six,
and can fit them, then I suggest four daylight and two
blue. Be sure to place the bulbs so that the colors blend
evenly... ie don't place the blue tubes next to each other
or too far apart. You are better off using tombstone ends

and ballasts purchased from a hardware store than the bulky rusty metal fluorescent light fixtures. Finally, if temperature is easy to control, you can enhance the light intensity with spotlights for a few hours a day. These must be sufficiently high above the tank... not in a closed canopy, since they do have the ability to heat up the tank very quickly. You are better off with more intense light sources, but you can have very good success still with a cheapie set up. Good luck!

Q. I've been reading your magazine for a couple of years now, and I was wondering about a particular aspect of biological filtration that I have never seen mentioned in any article. I'm a novice at fishkeeping and have only a rudimentary understanding of the particulars of biological filtration, but I do recall observing protozoa under a microscope when I was in grade school long ago; amoeba, paramecia, and flagella, among others. The protozoa we observed were from normal pond water.

If I remember correctly, the protozoa play an essential part in the pond's biological system. The articles I have read on biological filtration refer only to bacteria and not to protozoa, and, although protozoa are one-celled creatures, they are not classified as bacteria. I wanted to know whether they also play a part in aquarium biological filtration, whether the are also in saltwater systems, and whether the articles I have read intended to include the phylum protozoa when they used the word "bacteria."

Sincerely,

R. Darren Brewer,

Oklahoma City, OK

A. In fact, great number of mysteries may be the responsibility of protozoans. Sudden disappearance of algae, a tank's resistance to disease causing protozoans, a tank's tendency to accumulate... or not accumulate detritus are among the possibilities. But to answer your question, Darren, YES they do play a role in biological filtration, and you are very perceptive especially for a novice.

Authors referring to bacteria in the description of biological filtration are talking about nitrifying bacteria and heterotrophic bacteria only. They are not referring to protozoans. Protozoans accomplish a job like the heterotrophs, in that they break down organic matter, be it debris or soup, and liberate some ammonia in the process, which the nitrifying bacteria and algae further process. It is my belief that the difference between an "aged" aquarium and one which has merely been "cycled" is the presence of large, stable populations of heterotrophic bacteria and protozoans. In fact, I am certain that one of the principle features and benefits of live rock is the presence of unique protozoans from coral reefs, and of course these are involved in curing the rocks when they are first received. I am a novice on the subject of protozoans in the marine environment, but, like you, I am interested in what they do. I don't know how much spare time you have, or what you do for a living, but we could all sure afford to learn a little more about the functions of even a few little beasties... thanks for the comment Darren, and why don't you look into this some more, or at least get into the hobby?

Q. Dear Julian Sprung,
I have read "Reef Notes" and found in the February 1991 issue Lucas Alonso's letter. I was very impressed with what he said and I agree with him. I am 13 and have had no problems with my marine tank. I have now maintained a 30 gallon tank for 1 year without any trouble. I have 1 butterflyfish, 1 damsel, and 1 Moorish Idol. Why do people say they are hard to keep when they're not?

I have held live corals, sea anemones, and other delicate creatures, with no sign of stress at all! Even with my ammonia, nitrite, and nitrate high, my fish have lived for a year.

But let's get back to the topic. I went to a pet store in Florida where they wouldn't even let me buy a damsel because they thought I was too young. I don't like for people to act that way. But your editorials have inspired me, and gave me tips for keeping a better marine tank.

Thank you so much,
Patrick Drennen,
Ozark, AL.

P.S. Please print this in your next editorial.

A. Yes Sir!

Gee, I'd better watch out 'cause I might get overthrown from my post by this energetic kid. Thanks for the note, Patrick. I do have a couple of bones to pick with you, though. First, regarding Moorish Idols, I would not regard them as easy to keep, even though you are obviously having success with ONE SPECIMEN. I would say that they generally feed with gusto right away, often taking flake food within hours of introduction to an aquarium, but many people have difficulty maintaining them. Their longterm survival depends on good diet including lots of greens, compatible tank mates, and, usually, good water quality. They are prone to infections, which is the common cause for their demise. They like to cruise, and I must say that it is quite remarkable that yours is comfortable in a thirty gallon tank. Often, when they feel confined they have a habit of beating their mouths on the glass, and this can lead to a fatal infection. Although I agree you have the skill to create a healthy environment for your fish, I am glad that guy didn't let you buy the damsel because another damsel in your tank would surely have disrupted the balance of power. I suggest that if you want more fish you should set up another tank. I wouldn't mess around with the success of your thirty gallon environment. I am a bit puzzled about your comments about live corals and anemones, as I wonder what kind of butterflyfish you have that didn't bother them... there are a few species which do not bother corals and anemones. Also, I presume the bad water parameters were temporary.

Well, keep up the good work, and lighten up a little, ok guy? We all have much to learn from this hobby. If your enthusiasm remains, then maybe someday you'll be sharing your secrets with the rest of us.

June 1992   Bubble bath revisited

I want to add to my comments from last month's column regarding the bubble algae, *Ventricaria* and *Valonia* species. I mentioned that I suspected that sea urchins could eat and control them. In fact , they do. I tried the Pacific black long spined urchin, *Diadema* sp. and, although these are certainly undesirable bulldozers in a small reef aquarium, they really can consume the bubble algae, as well as tough green "brillo" turfs of *Cladophora* and *Cladophoropsis* species. If you have a problem with these algae you might employ an urchin as temporary cleanup, and remove it when the job is done... a task easier said than done... ouch!

Q. Dear Julian,
I have been reading and learning from your column for awhile now, and now I have several questions.

I am planning on painting the interior of my house in the near future. Knowing how the smell of paint affects ME, how will it affect my aquariums? How should I protect it from fumes, or do I just cover it with a drop cloth and hope for the best?

What is the advisable method for moving anemones? Do I just reach in and grab the little devil and hope I don't get stung? I don't want to expose them to the air at all, and while they don't move very quickly, I don't think netting them is the way to go about it.

Last question- My tank is set up near my living room window that gets some afternoon sunlight. Is it advisable to shut the tank lights off when the sunlight is hitting the tank? It doesn't get A LOT of sunlight- I live in the Pacific Northwest, where sunlight is a rare commodity 10 months out of the year.

Thank you so much for your attention.
Sincerely,
Michelle Blanchard,
Somewhere in the Pacific Northwest

A. Paint fumes are not really good for an aquarium, as you surmised. They're not as deadly as pesticide fumigation, however. Is it possible for you to leave the windows open to cross ventilate the house until the paint dries? At least that would reduce the concentration of fumes. A couple of strong air pumps located outside of your house, each equipped with a loooong airline, could be used to pump clean air into your canopy and your cabinet below the tank (if you have one). This would flush clean the air directly in contact with the water. Some combination of the above suggestions will work fine... the drop cloth idea isn't practical because the aquarium needs to breathe. The drop cloth would be useful to help prevent paint from getting on or in the aquarium.

Anemones are not as delicate as you believe. In fact, anemones are typically shipped "dry" (ie without water, though they are wet) from overseas in plastic bags. This technique not only saves on freight cost, but also improves survival, as it was discovered that anemones shipped submerged often suffocated. Lifting them out of water is harmless, so you are wrong about netting them, which is a safe practice. Of course the net must be washed thoroughly afterward to prevent injuring a netted fish with anemone slime and nematocysts. Some hobbyists use a plastic bag turned inside out to pick up anemones, in the same fashion as conscientious dog owners do with their pooch's feces, pulling them into the bag as it is turned "right side in." If you don't mind getting stung occasionally, or possibly damaging anemones by tearing the sticky tentacles, then you can just reach in and grab 'em with your bare hands. If the anemone is securely attached to the glass, a plastic credit card may be used like a spatula to lift (carefully!) a portion of the pedal disc. Once you've separated a "corner" of this foot from the glass, the rest should peel off if you carefully push it along. If the anemone is attached to a rock, it is best to move the rock and anemone together... anemones don't separate from rock as easily as they do from glass.

The only harm from sunlight in an aquarium is its ability to raise the temperature. If you use a chiller or this is not a problem, then by all means let it shine! Don't be silly, don't worry about your tank lights being on at the same time... leave them on. If the sunlight is direct, you probably will notice that it appears as if the lights aren't on anyway. A little sunlight goes a long way toward making photosynthetic creatures like your anemone(s) happy.

Q. Dear Julian,

I'm a huge fan, and cannot wait for my monthly copy to arrive. I find your articles interesting and to the point. My question deals with compatibility in the reef system. I have a 150 gallon tank, 250 lbs of live/plant rock, various types of *Caulerpa*, anemones, about 15 *Turbo* snails, and several invertebrates. Fish include a Flame Angel, Tomato Clown, two Percula Clowns, a few different gobies, and a Royal Gramma. I recently lost a Regal Angel due to what I believe is starvation. He never ate a bite and after seven weeks he became weak and died.

I wish to replace my lost angel with another hardier angel, namely an atlantic variety like a French or a Blue. But of the several people I have talked to, all have different stories as to its compatibility in a reef system. Also I'd like to put more than one pygmy angel in the same tank, but again I have been met with conflicting advice. Is there any publication that lists compatibility to reef systems, what kinds of fish do well in reef systems, feeding habits, suitable environment, etc.? Any suggestions would be greatly appreciated. Thanks, Ron Kastronis, Waldorf, MD.

A. Sorry to hear about your Regal Angel... as I mentioned in a previous column, the Philippine Regals have a poor survival record, and what you described is the exact fate for most of them, though sometimes a specimen will eat like gangbusters and live happily ever after. I feel that these should not be imported in large quantities... that they should be available upon request to those people who want them and are therefore prepared to keep them. The Red Sea and Indo Pacific variety, which has much richer coloration and a bright orange face, usually fares better in captivity... most of them will eat well if they haven't been damaged in transport, and they are compatible with corals, though it's always possible that the specimen you get will decide to eat the corals after all.

On that subject, your idea for a replacement does need more careful consideration, and you'll be glad that you wrote me. The Atlantic Blue Angel is a poor choice for a reef tank. At best it will be compatible with the corals and other inverts for a few months when it is small, but it will ultimately have a feast. Also, it will grow too large in proportion for your tank, and you will want to remove it one day. I recommend avoiding those fish which will have to be removed eventually, because they will be impossible to catch, and your goal should be to create a permanent environment for the specimens you buy. The French Angel, too, will ultimately grow really big. Small French Angels are real gems, with their pajama stripes and undulating "wag." They are also reasonably compatible with corals and other invertebrates. This one will have to be your decision. You will have to remove the french one day as it grows too large, but it is a nice fish when small, and it wouldn't be so difficult to catch, compared with most other fish. Remember that I never said it wouldn't bother your inverts. Most French Angels won't cause harm, but some will eat everything, and this is a characteristic of the pygmy angels as well. By the way, you can forget about your *Caulerpa* with a French Angel... it would surely decimate the plants.

You can put another pygmy angel or two in the tank with your Flame Angel, but he/she may beat the new ones up. They are likely to be accepted, however, so I'd give it a try. Avoid the Lemonpeel, which lives up to its reputation as a coral eater... a nice fish otherwise. You could try *C. acanthops, C. resplendens, C. argi, C. shepardi,* or *C. multicolor* (requires thick wallet).

As a matter of fact there is a good publication which will answer most of your fish compatibility and care questions, and I know that there are others coming soon. The only book which specifically focuses on the subject is *Fishes for the Invertebrate Aquarium*, 3rd edition, by Helmut Debelius. The English edition has been available for the past couple of years from Aquarium Systems. Another recent book, *The Reef Tank Owner's Manual*, by John Tullock, has an excellent chapter on fishes for the reef tank. It is published by Aardvark press. Both of these books should be available from your dealer.
I just returned home from an adventure with the San Francisco Aquarium Society. Quite a large group of enthusiastic hobbyists they are. Jeff Perrera and Wilfred Fong dragged, er, escorted me all over the place to see the top

reef tanks and some of the local stores. The tour was an enlightening experience for all, though a little tiring. The two nights of lecturing were well attended, and the crowd threw some challenging questions my way. Well, this weekend I'm off to New York for the lecture to the Brooklyn Aquarium Society, which means I have about enough time to change clothes and finish this column.

While I was in San Francisco, Jeff Schettler of Quality Aquatics informed me of a treatment he had routinely used successfully for the cure of "OOdinium" (*Amyloodinium Ocellatum*). That alone would be news, but he also had a special application of the treatment that worked safely in reef tanks. I was intrigued because I have seen whole tanks of fish lost to this dinoflagellate. The drug used in these applications is Metronidazole, a.k.a "Flagyl." This drug is used on people, so you should be able to get some through a pharmacist. I have not tried the treatment on a tank yet, but I trust these suggestions which Mr. Schettler kindly provided are correct.

Jeff commented that when treating or preventing this disease, as any other disease, it is important first to stabilize the fishes' physical environment, and correct sources of stress, including physical, chemical, and emotional.

To treat a regular fish tank, not a reef tank use 250-300 mg/ten gallons. Remove chemical filtration, ie. activated carbon. Signs of recovery should occur within 24 to 72 hours. A second dose may be administered on the third or fourth day, after a 25% water change. When siphoning out the water it is a good idea to siphon off exposed rock surfaces to remove parasites. After completing the treatment, filter the water with activated carbon to remove the medication.

Metronidazole may also be added to the food during the treatment. For reef tanks, the food treatment alone is the method Jeff recommended. Dissolve 250 mg of Metronidazole in one ounce of water, and add two or three tablespoons of freeze dried food, ie. Euphasiids. Feed this food exclusively for a week to ten days. The only negative effect that Jeff has noticed in invertebrates is the loss of crowns by feather dusters. After the treatment period, perform a water change and filter with activated carbon.

Have you seen the March issue of Audubon Magazine? The cover story by Mark Derr is entitled "Raiding The Reefs," and it is not a very pretty article, certainly not a kind one to the aquarium industry and marinelife fishermen. This article is a carefully planned, appropriately timed, and intentionally twisted piece of work based somewhere between fact and fiction. Mr. Derr is a very creative writer. Of course a publication like Audubon magazine cannot take responsibility for the opinions of a single author, and certainly an author's opinions do not reflect any kind of position taken by the Audubon society as a whole. Nevertheless, the article deserves a substantial level of criticism and, to be fair in presenting a truly objective view of the situation, Audubon magazine should allow equal time and space in its pages for rebuttal. At the very least, I think it should publish photographs of my aquaria which were taken by a photographer that Audubon hired. I believe the magazine did not use the photos in the original article since they did not match the negative impression of the hobby, and they proved the so-called "claims and assertions" I made in the article. The photos conflicted with Mr. Derr's use of words in the attempt to throw a shadow of doubt on my credibility. Furthermore, Mr. Derr flat out lied when he wrote that I could not provide documented proof of corals spawning and completing a life cycle in an aquarium. In fact, the documentation, including photographs, was offered to him and was not accepted. Mr. Derr does not consider publication in an Aquarium journal valid proof of anything.

I spent the a day with Mr. Derr and another day with the photographer because I felt that I might be able to give some valuable input on both the positive and the negative sides of our hobby. I knew that the article was not going to be a glowing report. Still, I expected the article to dig deeper. I really thought Mr. Derr would pull through and offer some insight instead of resorting to incitation with no acceptable solution.

Instead of attacking our hobby and industry, why can't

Audubon and other environmental groups WORK WITH US to create a system of regulation and sound planning? Wouldn't it be more productive to work together toward a common goal? After all, aren't we really on the same side? I KNOW the aquarium industry and hobbyists are concerned about the reefs, the ocean, and the planet. I wonder if many environmental groups really exist only for the cause and the funding it brings. I don't think that Audubon falls under this category. A lot of hobbyists and aquarium industry people are members of Audubon. I think that together we can achieve action, but as rivals we waste our creative resources, and sabotage the goal of actually doing something for the environment. If you feel the need to write your opinion after reading the article in Audubon magazine, please be sure to offer constructive input, and by all means let them know the success you are having with your corals. Input on the scope and outlook for improvement regarding harmful fishing practices and regulation of shipping and handling techniques are also welcome. Perhaps the article in question will at least serve to get people in our industry agitated enough to act, which would be a nice result, but I don't think that a deliberately inaccurate report is justified by even such a good end.

July 1992

For all the people who have written asking about how to move a tank, this column is for you, but first...

No more chowder, this wrasse chows down on clam eaters.

Jeff at H$_2$O Tropicals reported to me that sixline wrasses, *Pseudocheilinus hexataenia*, eat the tiny white pyramidellid snails that parasitize *Tridacna* clams.
Thanks for the tip, Jeff!

Q. Dear Julian
This December we will be entering our fifteenth year as marine aquarium hobbyists. We have two 55 gallon tanks, one established in 1980 and the other in 1984. Both tanks are doing very well, equipped with an oversized canister filter, protein skimmer, undergravel filter, and a combination of an actinic and "reeflite" lamps. A 15% water change is made every two weeks or so. Each tank is fed on average once a day with either a brand

name flake food or frozen brine shrimp. Each tank has some live rock, mushroom and leather corals purchased over the years, several anemones and plenty of places for the seven to eight fish to take refuge in. The tanks are doing well enough that the thrill of adding new fish to the tanks happens maybe twice a year. Long time residents include a ten year old Seabae Clown, two seven year old Tomato Clowns, a seven year old carpet anemone, an eleven year old hermit crab, a pygmy and Bicolor Angel in the 5 to 6 year old range.

Our problem is, we will be moving half way across the country this summer. Do we have to sell off our friends? We have moved across town successfully, but never over such a long distance. Immediately upon arrival we plan on setting up one 135-150 gallon tank. Can we successfully move most of the inhabitants? I remember when we first set up the tanks it seemed to take several months before we could start adding fish. I know things have progressed over the years, how should we proceed? Sincerely, Michael and Marcia Sandstrom, Marlborough, NH

A. It sounds like the two of you are not at odds over the fish and their priority in the scheme of things, which is definitely to both of your advantages especially now as you contemplate a big move. Two 55 gallon tanks are not too difficult to move, even if it's a couple thousand miles. I presume you will be driving with most of your belongings to your new residence. You did not indicate exactly how far your move was, or how many days you planned to be in transit, but assuming you are a motivated couple, I estimate your trip "half way across the country" will take two days. If this is the case, then the packing method with oxygen which I will describe is definitely the way to do it. If your trip will take three full days or longer, then you must consider a few alternatives which I will shortly describe.

Whatever truck/trailer you use, be sure to leave room for your tanks and about eight to ten 17"x17"x10" styrofoam boxes. You can purchase these from your fish dealer who gets them with every fish shipment. Your dealer's cost is about five dollars per box and, since they are used, he shouldn't charge any more than this. You may use other containers for the move, but I prefer the styrofoam boxes for their insulating ability. You will also need plastic bags for packing the fish, plenty of rubberbands, and oxygen. Hopefully you have good relations with a shop owner who can help you with the packing equipment. Use larger bags than usual for the size of the specimen, and purchase three bags per specimen. You will be double-bagging things, and the third bag is kept in store as leak insurance. You should pack only one fish to a bag, but you may pack many compatible invertebrates in the same bag. The first step in preparing your specimens for the move will be difficult for you both, but it is one of the most important steps, so DON'T BREAK THE RULES. You must not feed the fish for four days prior to the move. Don't feed them at all, I said. This will prevent them from polluting the water they will reside in during transit, and will slow their metabolism down. You indicated a 15% water change per two weeks. Keep up this routine, even before the big move. If the schedule has you making a water change just a few days before the move, don't do any major vacuuming or disturbing of the environment...just siphon out and replace the 15%.

Count on the packing and moving procedure for the tank to take three times as long as you expect. If you plan to leave first thing in the morning, one of you will be up for most of the night. You should have most of your belongings packed already before beginning on the tank.

You might be wondering what to do with the living gravel from your undergravel filter. For this you need full size packing bags. The gravel will be packed damp, but not submerged. Place the gravel into buckets and pour off as much water as possible without dumping the gravel onto the floor and making a mess. Scoop out the gravel into an open, full size bag sitting in a styrofoam box. Pour out any remaining water from the scoop before putting the gravel in the bag. Once you've got about 30 lbs of damp gravel in the box, if you have the oxygen cylinder handy, go ahead and fill the bag with O_2 and close it tight with a rubberband. It can be kept live like this for several days. If you will be transporting the box to a place with an O_2 cylinder, simply close the bag to prevent the remaining water on the gravel from evaporating until you get there. You do not need to transport all of

the gravel this way. One thirty pound box per tank is all
that you need to keep "live" in a bag with oxygen. The
rest can be placed damp in a large bucket. DO NOT
RINSE THE GRAVEL TO CLEAN IT. You may feel a
strong urge to flush out the dirt you see when you are
pouring off the excess water, but don't do it! This dirt
(actually all the little "bugs" on it) is what will afford
your aquariums instant stability when you set them back
up at the new location.

At the new location. . . after you have made new saltwater and set the tanks up with the spare gravel which was
not packed with oxygen, and allowed the water to circu-
late for about half an hour, you can add the live gravel,
and allow the tank to clear. Be sure that the temperature
and specific gravity are about the same in the new water
and the old water that your pets are packed in. Next place
the rocks, coral, and inverts in the tank, with the exception of shrimps which should be treated like fish, but
acclimated separately from them as follows. When you
arrive it is essential that you slowly allow the fishes' (and
any pet shrimps') water to equilibrate with atmospheric
CO_2. In transit the CO_2 builds up in the water, causing the
pH to fall. If you were to place the fishes right into the
tank they would probably go into shock and die.

What you do is to place the fishes in their old water into
a large bucket(s) and administer a light stream of air
from an airstone and pump. This is the way the fish
importers usually do it when they receive fish from overseas. After about an hour of this light aeration, use a
length of airline hose compressed with a C-clamp to
slowly siphon a trickle flow of new aquarium water into
the buckets of fish, allowing the waters to mix. Maintain
light aeration through this whole procedure. During this
procedure it is important to keep the buckets covered to
prevent the fish from jumping, fighting, and to minimize
fright from bright lights. After the volume of water that
the fish are in is about half old and half new (at least),
you may re-introduce them into their tanks. The tank
lights should be off and the room lights should be on so
that the fish are neither startled nor blind. You should
use the plastic bags to catch and move the fish to their
tanks, and add back the water siphoned out.

If your trip will take three full days or longer, or if you simply haven't got the room for all of this fish stuff, then you can pack the fish and inverts as described, and send them by air freight to someone who can receive them and care for them in a holding facility. A pet store or hobbyist could perform this service for you. I'd recommend avoiding this alternative if possible, because it is both risky and costly, but you may not have a choice. The gravel would not need to be sent by air as it can last nicely for several days in transit. You might also consider only bringing those pets which you couldn't bear to part with, and selling the ones you could easily replace. This would certainly lighten the load. It is also possible to transport fish and invertebrates in aerated buckets, with no need for packing and oxygen, just a battery operated air pump that can plug into your car's cigarette lighter. I prefer the packing method, but I want to offer at least one alternative for you. I hope the move is not too traumatic. Be sure to plan everything in advance so that you can be prepared to handle the unexpected things which will surely happen.

Q. I am currently having problems with two of my invertebrates. First, in early December, 1991 I purchased two giant clams. One has a pink mantle and the other has a deep purple mantle with bright blue polka dots. After six weeks the purple clam began developing pale areas in the mantle. At that time I changed my lighting from one 30 watt actinic 03, one 30 watt actinic white and one 15 watt Triton to two 175 watt metal halides (5500k). I was careful to expose the tank to the halides for short periods of time at first, increasing to the current twelve hour on/off schedule for almost four weeks and the clam shows no signs of slowing or reversing its loss of zooxanthellae. The clam also does not appear to be opening quite as far as it used to. The halides are fan cooled and do not seem to be causing any temperature problems. All of the other tank inhabitants are doing well and showing growth, including the other clam. What are your suggestions for saving this clam?
The second problem: My leather coral was also added in Dec 1991. It has been growing steadily, is budding new little leather corals, and has firmly attached itself to the

live rock that I placed it on. During the last several weeks it developed a white area on its oral disc that has progressed to a hole through the disc. The hole is small, and is not enlarging, but it also is not showing any signs of healing. I am careful to rinse away any debris that settles on the coral with a baster. Should I expect the hole to heal itself over time or should I do something to help the coral beat this infection? (I do not believe any of the fish are munching on the coral). Laura Green, member eastern Iowa Aquarium Association, Iowa City, IA

A. The bleaching or loss of zooxanthellae in your purple *Tridacna maxima* clam is probably an indication that it is adapting to the changes in the light field which it has experienced since capture. These clams are photosynthetic, and depend on intense light for their food. The fact that it is not opening like it used to, however, is a very bad sign. When I see a clam behaving this way I promptly move it to a new location. It is possible that a predator (worm, mantis shrimp, carnivorous snail) is irritating it at its present location, and moving it would provide relief. Sometimes a clam may slide a little from the original position, causing a chronic tugging on the byssus threads that attach it to the rock. This situation is tiring to the clam, and can weaken it. Be sure that adjacent corals are not stinging the clam. Watch the fish very carefully. Centropyge angels are very sneaky about picking on clams. Clams can get infections which are often lethal in a very short time, so you must act quickly if they are not opening properly.

It is possible that a depleted trace element such as iodine or iron is a contributing factor... be sure to keep up with additions. The clams also require calcium and strontium to form their shell... be sure to keep the calcium level up above 400 ppm, and add strontium according to the directions of commercially available solutions, or, if you make your own, add approximately 2 milliliters of a 10% aqueous solution of strontium chloride per 25 gallons per two weeks.

What you are witnessing in your leather coral is actually a form of asexual reproduction. The species you have develops necrotic "spots" as you described, near the edge of the crown. They may be produced by infections or protozoans, but these are not necessarily the cause. After a hole has formed, it may erode slowly lengthwise so that a portion of the edge of the crown becomes separated and falls off, producing a new leather coral. It is a good idea to clean necrotic areas with a few squirts of water from a baster, but don't worry too much about your specimen, I'm sure it's fine.

I am amused at your reference to the creature's "oral disc." Of course you know that these soft corals don't actually have an oral disc. The mouths are on the individual polyps. Sometimes a leather coral will develop what looks like a mouth on the crown. This usually occurs when the coral has been cut or injured near the center (away from the edges) of the crown, and what happens is that during the healing process, especially if some algae or gravel enters the depression, some of the exposed tissue inside the wound differentiates into smooth, un-polyped column tissue... a bald spot. If the algae grows there the leather coral may form a gall around it, and the resulting elevation and smooth interior gives the impression of a mouth.

Dear Julian,

Q. I have had problems with my marine tank from the start. I have had freshwater tanks for years but my problems lie in the salt water. The set up is as follows: 50 gallon tank, fluval 303 canister filter, about 21/2 inches of Florida crushed coral, U.G. filter with 2 Hagen 402 power heads, & lighting, my problem area. I've tried everything under the sun including: standard aquarium lights, plant "gro" bulbs (which I've found to work the best when I wasn't keeping anemones), to Ultra lumes, Actinic 03, and Actinic Days. All I was getting in the tank was this rusty orange-brown coloring in the water. Not attached to anything just suspended in the water, it got to the point where when I'd look down the end of my 48 inch tank, I could only see maybe five inches in, it was so dense. Finally, after 7-8 months of this I was given a protein skimmer and all of my problems were solved! So I thought...

The tank has been set up for a year and a half now and I can't seem to get any green growing in it, good or bad. Even when I tried to seed the tank with various plants and green algae they just turned brown within a day or two and withered away. The only time I had any green in the tank was with the Gro bulbs. I presently have one Actinic 03 and one Actinic-Day, both 48 inches and still get only brown. I do a 25% water change per month and monitor all levels with a SeaTest multi-kit. Everything is always what it should be. Finally, what I have in the tank: one Blue Tang, one Mandarin Goby, four Percula Clowns, 2 Lemon Gobies, one Neon Goby, one black urchin, one Arrow Crab, one anemone crab, one six-inch and one two-inch anemone. I don't over feed, and leave the lights on for about fifteen hours a day. I have talked to people from coast to coast and no one has been able to help yet. Please help! Still no green, Dina L. Fontana, Warren, MI

A. First, let me remind you that your immediate problem is more conceptual than actual, though to set you on the right course you will need to make both conceptual and actual changes. What's all of this philosophical sounding nonsense, you wonder. Well, I'm amused that the good guy, bad guy story with regard to the color of algae persists among fishkeepers. While one can make a good argument over the relative "badness!" of a particular type of algae in a reef tank because of the alga's ability to smother invertebrates, in a fish-only system the color of the algae is purely an argument of aesthetics, and one should not place any moral judgment on the presence of one type of algae or another. The algae bloom in the water which your tank initially experienced was definitely a "bad" situation because of its less than desirable aesthetic appeal and potentially toxic effect on the fish. Such blooms can rapidly deplete oxygen at night, elevate pH during the day, and may give off toxic compounds in the water. I suspect the cause of the bloom was some nutrient(s) in the freshwater you are using. I expect that you are using raw tap water, and there is a change that you need to make. I am amazed how often hobbyists overlook the tap water as a possible source of problems. The use of a good reverse osmosis or a deionization system will effectively remove the majority of phosphates. nitrates, silicate, and heavy metals that can cause algae blooms. Shop around for a good unit, and get one for your own health as well as your fishes'.

Another problem is your 15 hour day length. Ten to twelve hours is better. I know you like to see your fish after you come home from work. Well, use a timer to turn the lights on a little later and leave them on for twelve hours at most.

If you want to grow *Caulerpa* species, or other macroalgae, your success will be limited by the grazing of your blue tang and the sea urchin. These two guys definitely are playing a role in the appearance of your tank right now. They are nice pets, don't get me wrong, but don't feel bad about the type and color of the algae in your aquarium as long as everybody else is healthy. On the subject of healthy fish, I'm glad you are using the skimmer. . . keep on using it. Be patient. It sounds like your tank is now progressing well, and with the changes I suggest, I'm sure your level of satisfaction will increase.

That's a wrap.

August 1992

Q. Dear Don
I've been in the marine hobby for about two years and have been quite successful at maintaining a fish only aquarium. I'm about to convert a 30 gallon "long" aquarium to a reef tank and desperately need your advice.

This is how I envision my set up. The bottom of the tank will be bare with the exception of 1/3 base rock and 2/3 live rock. A large wet/dry (made for tanks in the 100 gallon range) which should mature the live rock in two weeks. Two pumps will run the dual feed back to the tank. A protein skimmer will be added when I start to introduce my pets. The lighting will consist of two actinic blues and one actinic white. One Actinic 03 will run from 7 a.m. to 10 p.m. and the other actinics from 8 a.m. to 9 p.m. I don't intend to feed the tank except for the normal reef additives and an occasional treat of brine shrimp.

I plan to stock the tank with two flower anemones, various coral polyps, one or two soft corals, brown and purple mushrooms, curliques, a cleaner shrimp, a camel back shrimp, two small starfish, a small Coral Beauty, a Flame Hawk and a Royal Gramma and finally a heavy growth of *Caulerpa*. Invertebrates will be stocked first, fish last.

This is where you come in. Am I allowing enough time for the live rock to mature? Is my lighting combination too strong or too weak for that size tank and the inverts? Can you recommend the common names of some hardy soft corals and starfish for a beginner? I've received mixed reviews on whether carpet anemones are good reef pets (the issue is whether they move around alot), what do you recommend?

I believe your advice is invaluable and look forward to hearing from you. Sincerely, Michael Donaldson, Kettering, MD.

A. Don passed this letter on to me, and I thought it covered a number of issues that I could discuss for the benefit of the readers.

It sounds like you know someone who has filled your head with some absolutes about reef keeping, Michael. Don't be caught up by inflexible technique.
You don't have to use 1/3 base rock, but your decision to do so may be an economic one, and that I understand. I prefer to use 100% live rock. Whatever rock you choose, be sure to pick interesting shapes to allow the proper loose, open stacking which assists water flow and prevents excessive detritus accumulation. Use plastic cable ties to secure the rocks into a structure... a drill and masonry bit may be necessary to make holes in the rock.

A biological filter will not mature the rocks. The bacteria and microorganisms on the rocks themselves will break down any fouling matter from plants and invertebrates that died in transit. This process takes two to three weeks, but it is best to be patient when first making the reef tank, and wait a month or more before adding fishes. It is not necessary to do so, just better.

You don't need such a large wet/dry filter. You should leave more room and money for a good protein skimmer.

Regarding the lights you chose, I recommend one more bulb with daylight color temperature, for a total of four bulbs at least over your twelve inch wide tank. If you can manage six bulbs, it would be better. If you can incorporate the polished aluminum reflectors now available, do so. Your planned photoperiod is too long. The total time the lights are on should not exceed twelve hours.

Regarding feeding, it is always best to be conservative, but beware of getting into the habit of starving your fish! Your Gramma and Flame Hawk will need to be fed at least three times per week, preferably with a greater variety of foods than just brine shrimp.

On your selection of specimens, a few words of caution come to mind. I gather that you have seen the species you mentioned and are attracted by their appearance, but you have chosen some invertebrates that may not be compatible. Large anemones do move around a lot, and in a 30 gallon tank this would surely shorten the lifespan of most corals you planned to keep. Curlique anemones are fascinating and their partnership with pistol shrimp and *Periclimenes* shrimp is worthy of a display tank, but this anemone is a 'mover and a stinger' too, and it is also adept at snaring fish that wander in the night.

I'm not sure which shrimp you mean by "camel back," though I suspect it is a *Rhynchocinetes* sp. or possibly a *Saron* sp. Either of these may decide to munch on corals or anemones, so beware. Sometimes they do no harm, but then other times... If you like shrimp, stick with *Lysmata amboinensis*, the scarlet cleaner shrimp, or *Stenopus hispidus*, the banded-coral shrimp. You can try *Lysmata debelius*, the blood shrimp, if you can afford it, or the common peppermint shrimp from the Caribbean, which is also a *Lysmata* sp.* If you are fortunate enough to find one, the interesting "sexy" shrimp, *Thor amboinensis*, makes a fine pet, and it will live among the tentacles of your coral or anemones. Whatever shrimp you choose, be sure to acclimate it slowly, as shrimps have a habit of going into shock and dying when improperly handled. A freshwater dip as a precautionary measure will almost certainly prove fatal to the shrimp, so don't even think of doing it.

* *Lysmata wurdemani* from the Caribbean has been observed feeding on small polyped stony corals (ie. *Acropora, Pocillopora* spp.) on occasion. It can do some harm to branch tips, but it seldom kills a colony.

This past weekend, as I was lecturing for the Bucks County Aquarium Society, a member of the club asked me about freshwater dips for shrimp, as he had read in a book that any shrimp or crustacean should be dipped in freshwater

*Star Polyps are actually *Pachyclavularia* spp., and this name will likely be considered a synonym of *Briareum*. "Clove Polyps" are *Clavularia* spp.

before being introduced into the aquarium, to kill parasites. My eyes opened wide as he told me this, and I responded "DON'T DO IT!" Well, he had already tried it, and yes, the shrimp promptly died. Crustaceans, especially shrimps, are extremely sensitive to changes in osmotic pressure. I can't imagine why the author had suggested dipping them, unless he was referring to crustaceans intended as live food for the fish, and not crustaceans as pets.

If you wish to keep some small starfish, avoid the chocolate chip star which will eat whatever it can sit on. The blue *Linkia* star is a good choice, but be sure that it is healthy! It must be crawling on the glass or trucking along on the rocks when you buy it. Also beware of the little parasite which looks like a blue shell attached to the arm(s) of the star... it is about 1/4 inch in diameter and not very conspicuous... usually it is on the underside if present, and it can be removed with a tweezers. The tiny red *Fromia* stars also make fine pets, but must not be kept in a packing bag too long, nor exposed to temperature extremes, and they must be acclimated to the aquarium. If they are improperly handled they literally disintegrate. Serpent stars are interesting, hardy, beautiful, and compatible, so I guess you might want a few.

You asked about hardy soft corals. Most soft corals are quite hardy, though there are some exceptions. For the beginner, I recommend such un-killables as Leather coral (*Sarcophyton* spp.), Finger leather (*Lobophytum* spp.), *Sinularia* spp., and "star polyps" (*Clavularia* * sp.). All of these like strong currents, and tolerate a wide range of light regimes.

Q. Dear Julian
About a month ago I decided to become a serious reef keeper. What I did not realize was the magnitude of the hobby. I've been reading for a month and am beginning to get a grip on some of it. I have the Moe books and acquired your tape. Your tape was wonderful and is exactly what I had in mind when I decided to do this. From books and magazines I sort of know what I need, but what are the best products. There are 100's to chose from. There is also some conflicting information to cloud the issue. The expertise and availability in my area is limited,

therefore some product evaluation and names of quality suppliers of livestock would be appreciated. Advertising can be misleading and there is so much of it...who knows.

I'm pretty handy and would attempt to build my own filters and skimmers. Which plans available are of quality engineering principals and work? Only about a hundred to choose from.

The one thing I have done is to purchase a 100 gallon acrylic tank in Seattle. I'm in the process of acquiring the books from Mr. Thiel. on reef keeping. Thanks for your time and consideration. Sincerely, D.M. Foster, BC Canada

A. You can imagine I get a lot of letters like yours. The best I can do for you is to tell you to join an aquarium society or two. These offer the perfect opportunity to get unbiased opinion about equipment and technique from hobbyists who are actually keeping aquaria and using the equipment you are wondering about. Clubs also have handy members like you who design and build their own equipment. Please understand that my purpose in this column is to help you develop proper technique, to troubleshoot mysterious problems, and explain the biology of the reef and organisms on it. I try to bring you up to speed with the latest technology and methods, but to make Reef Notes a product review column would sacrifice the objectivity of the information presented. I will occasionally review a book or product that Don Dewey sends me, but this is done apart from Reef Notes. Please refer to the readers exchange and the occasional society listings for club contact information.

Q. Dear Julian
I would like to comment on "hobbyist research" and scientific community research in aquarium science. Perhaps what the U.P. Aquarium Society (UPAS) has done may be a good example how hobbyists and the academe may interface in aquarium science.

It's true that many hobbyists consider aquarium keeping just a hobby. The same is true with us in the UPAS where most of the members are hobbyists, although some are professional marine scientists. However, being hobbyists we make it a point that our members be scientifically oriented when doing research in aquarium science. We hope in the future that our work will be good enough to be published in a scientific journal and the aquarium magazines.

The scientific community is not very aware of the developments in aquarium science. This is because aquarists do not publish in journals. However, if hobbyists are serious enough to pursue lines of research, a good idea is to interface with an academic institution. Being an organization based in a university, UPAS has been actively cooperating and interfacing with the University of the Philippines Marine Science Institute (UPMSI) on developments in marine and aquarium science. UPAS has gained interesting ideas for hobbyist investigations in marine science, while it has provided important insights to faculty members of UPMSI on coral reef aquariums and their role in ecological modeling. For example, we have documented the first natural spawning of Tridacnid clams in a closed aquarium system in the Philippines. Another field for useful interfacing is the problem of cyanide fishing. UPAS has provided insights from the hobbyist point of view to marine scientists.

UPAS has developed its own coral reef aquariums which are modifications of natural systems. We are in the process of developing algal scrubber systems for home aquariums. These are coupled to undergravel filter systems. The wet-dry filter system as practiced in the USA is impractical for the Philippines, as it is too expensive. In all these efforts, marine scientists have been very helpful.

At present, we are very much involved in research on cyanide fishing. This is a problem that is critical for the Philippine tropical fish industry.

UPAS has a goal of increasing the hobbyist's competency in science. For us, aquarium keeping is an extension of our education.
Interested People can contact:
UPAS c/o Benjamin Vallejo, Jr. U.P. Marine Science

Institute, University of the Philippines
Diliman, Quezon City 1101, Republic of the Philippines

Sincerely Yours, Benjamin M. Vallejo, Jr. President UPAS

A. Thanks for your comments, Benjamin. I am encouraged by you group's efforts on the cyanide issue. In your reef filtration efforts I suggest you work on developing good protein skimmers which can be made easily and inexpensively from PVC pipe. The algal scrubbers are interesting, but are not as useful as protein skimming for maintaining live corals. *Tridacna* clams typically spawn in aquariums when they are stressed. It is important to remove the clam when it releases gametes into the water, as the concentration in a closed system can kill the clam and other tank inhabitants. As you are aware I'm sure, there are numerous commercial projects now spawning and rearing *Tridacna* clams. Some work is being done now in the Philippines, and you might want to "interface" with such a project. The library at your University should have lots of info on giant clam farming. Best wishes to you.

Q. Dear Julian,
My husband Arnold and I are newcomers to the aquarium hobby. Thus far, we have only kept freshwater fish but we are beginning to dream about the next step: a saltwater tank. However, we feel somewhat intimidated by the variety of gadgets and opinions relating to saltwater aquariums. Perhaps you would set us straight and describe how we should proceed so that any loss of animal life would be minimized.

What sort of tank are we thinking about? There is only one fish that we would like to keep, a moray eel. On the other hand, from various sources (including J. Tullock's "Manual"), we have gathered that a good place to start for a reef aquarium would be a deep (or cave) reef. Is it possible to mix these ideas, ie. can one have a deep reef with one moray eel? What size tank would be optimal? Can we just convert one of our 55 gallon tanks? Which of the moray eels would be most suitable?

I remember reading that moray eels are hardy (a plus) but do best if the water temperature is about 79 degrees farenheight. Deep reefs, on the other hand, require water temperatures near 75 degrees. Is this temperature variation too much? Would a chiller be necessary or advisable? (That leads to another question: what gadgetry would be optimal? a trickle filter? protein skimmer? UV sterilizer? R.O. unit?)

How would you start a reef tank of the above sort? Is there such a thing as "live deep rock" or are we supposed to use whatever live rock we can find? Are there light requirements for the live rock?

At what point would you introduce the eel? Once the invertebrates are in place or earlier? Which species of inverts would be optimal, given the eel?

Finally, is it possible to move a reef tank? There is a chance that we might move within a year. Should we wait and set up the tank only after we know where we are going to live?

Arnold and I hope that you will not find our questions too trivial. We are greatly interested in the aquarium hobby but we wish to do things the right way without unnecessary loss of life. Perhaps you could give us a blue-print for the continuation of our voyage. With many thanks, Arja H. Turunen-Red, Austin, TX

A. It is possible to have a moray eel with invertebrates, as you hope to do. By deep reef you mean low light reef. The depth of the tank, then, makes no difference. You can use a 55 gallon tank, though I think that a wider tank, such as a 75 gallon, or a 50 gallon breeder offers much greater potential for creating a realistic, cave or grotto display. In a 55 gallon tank you are practically forced to build a vertical wall of rock along the back. In a wider tank you can incorporate the sides for the illusion of depth. I recommend that you use at least four fluorescent tubes that each span the tank length. If you can fit more, do so. Incorporate two or more blue tubes for the deep sea effect, and the benefit to the photosynthetic life on the rocks.

Choose rock with encrusting pink and purple coralline algae. It will adapt well to the lower light levels. Tie the rocks together with plastic cable ties to create a secure structure with caves that won't collapse on your eel. Use a drill and masonry bit if necessary, to make holes for the plastic ties.

If you wish to use a wet/dry filter for this tank, be sure to modify the surface skimmer to prevent your pet eel from taking a trip over the falls. You can also just run this tank with an undergravel filter, either reverse flow or just with airlifts or powerheads. Really, the choice is yours, this is a simple set-up. I definitely recommend a protein skimmer for any marine aquarium. The U.V. sterilizer is not necessary, but would do no harm, and if it makes you sleep easier, then use it. I believe in using purified water, so yes, an R.O. filter on your tap is a good idea... for your health too.

The tank should have a cover which prevents the eel from wandering out and about in your living room. Imagine the squishy encounter as you make your way to the fridge for a midnite bite and meet up with your pet eel on his way back with a beer and an open can of sardines, only he can't make it back because he's dried up and stuck to the carpet, the beer is spilled, and gravity works different outside of water, or so he says. A secure lid is a must with eels.

If you can maintain the tank at 80 degrees or less, and the temperature is pretty stable (plus or minus one degree), then you don't need a chiller for this set up.

To create this tank I would set it up and get the water circulating. Purchase all of the live rock at once, build the reef structure using cable ties, and allow the rock to develop purifying populations of bacteria and microorganisms for about three weeks. During this period I would monitor the water for ammonia and nitrite, and I would expect to get a significant reading for both initially. When there is no ammonia or nitrite after about three weeks, it is safe to add the eel or other invertebrates. It doesn't hurt to wait longer, and it is always best to add the invertebrates slowly, building up a nice population. Avoid crustaceans that might pick on the eel or get eaten by it. I think that a bed of mushroom anemones and several leather corals would make a nice display.

For info on the insanity of reef tank transportation, please refer to last month's column. I can't tell you whether to wait or build the tank now. I don't know how crazy you are.

Q. Dear Julian,
I have been plagued by slime algae: Red has shown up in small patches, but the brown covers my glass as fast as I can wipe it off. The brown slime algae almost appears as a smudge, not a patch....

Chris Bach, Stamford, CT

A. I have much abbreviated Chris' letter. Usually golden brown sheet and slime algae are diatoms which are limited by the presence of silicate which they use to build their skeleton. Chris indicated in his letter that he was using deionized water, and while it is possible that these are diatoms that are causing the frustration he is experiencing, I suspect they may be a type of dinoflagellate which occasionally blooms miserably in reef aquaria, and the causative agent remains a mystery. The description of a smudge like appearance is characteristic. Oxygen bubbles trapped in the mush is also typical with these as it is with cyanobacteria. One definitive quality of the dinoflagellate bloom is that it is toxic to some invertebrates and fish...specifically those which ingest it. Snails appear to be paralyzed by the stuff. They will drop off the rocks and "hang out" on the bottom of the tank, upside-down.

Tangs seem to suffer from eating the dinoflagellates, and may waste away as a result. Most interestingly, sea urchins are also affected which leads me to an important hypothesis: It is possible that the mass die-off of *Diadema* urchins in the Caribbean in the 1980's was caused by toxic dinoflagellates growing epiphytically on the algae and seagrass being grazed by the urchins. The

*If dinoflagellates did cause the die off of the urchins, it is possible that the introduction to the Caribbean was from a ship that may have carried it from another ocean, possibly via the Panama canal.

**In volume one of this series and in *The Reef Aquarium* Vol. One. There are additional recommendations for the control of dinoflagellates. One of the best cures seems to be boosting the pH with Kalkwasser additions. See this books for further explanation.

manner in which the urchins died is the same as occurs in an aquarium afflicted with a dinoflagellate bloom.* Blooms may occur naturally in nature, governed by the availability of limiting nutrients, but it is also possible that some man-made pollution stimulated a bloom. I am curious about the impact of heavy metals, among other things, on algae growth.

The only good news I can offer regarding dinoflagellate blooms** in the aquarium is that they go away suddenly... the bloom crashes when the nutrients are used up. I don't know what the key element that limits them is, however. I advise boosting the protein skimming and performing water changes using purified water for the mix in order to starve them. Regular cleaning of the mechanical filter(s) helps remove trapped dinoflagellates and thus slowly removes the critical element. The use of an ultraviolet sterilizer may also help curtail the bloom. It is important to avoid adding substances which are known to stimulate plant growth when such a bloom afflicts the tank. These would include vitamins, iron, and molybdenum. Such additions are beneficial when the tank is not experiencing a problem. Be patient, the bloom will go away. I will have more to say about this subject in the future. In the meantime, don't go around worrying that your tank has this problem. Diatoms are far more common and are easily controlled by limiting the addition of silicate with filtered make-up water.

October 1992

The recommendations I gave a few months ago for the use of metronidazole (aka Flagyl) in the treatment of *Amyloodinium* need to be revised. Jeff Schettler of Quality aquatics, who advised me of this treatment, now has additional information which indicates that not all forms of metronidazole are effective in the treatment of Amyloodinium. The preferred form of the drug is pure crystalline product. It appears that only uncut, USDA metronidazole works in the dosage given, which is 25 to 30 milligrams per gallon for treating a fish tank. When the disease incidence is in a reef aquarium, the treatment should be added to the food only, by dissolving 300 mg of metronidazole in one ounce of pure water and soaking dried food in it. This treated food should be the only food offered. Other forms of metronidazole which are available in tablet form for treatment of pets and humans are cut with binders which release the metronidazole only at the low pH inside the gut. Jeff informs me that he is preparing an article on this treatment. He also informed me that pure metronidazole is available from Seachem.

Jeff also mentioned that the International Marinelife Alliance (IMA) was implementing the use of ion-specific cyanide testing in the Philippines with the help of a grant from the Philippine government, and simultaneously starting another net training program for collectors. A cyanide detection test (CDT) laboratory will be set up in Manila, staffed by personnel from the Bureau of Fisheries and Aquatic Resources (BFAR). IMA has arranged to have Dr. R. Soundararajan, who developed the test, visit Manila to train the BFAR personnel. According to plan, after a grace period, the CDT procedure will ensure that only exporters with net-caught marines will be able to obtain export permits from BFAR.

Other contributors to this project are the Pet Care Trust and the Osborne Laboratory of the New York Aquarium.

Let's hope this plan works! It sounds like the most encouraging news yet on this subject. Further plans for the use of testing here in the USA by hobbyists and businesses should really help make it possible to eliminate the cyanide problem. Ignorance is the only stumbling block that needs to be overcome...I think it will take a great deal of p.r. work to make new hobbyists aware, and testing must be easily available to offer any hope of getting a handle on the situation from this end. The Philippines are not the only locale for cyanide fishing.

Q. Dear Julian,
This letter is in regards to your comments in the Reef Notes Section of the June 1992 issue of FAMA. I would first like to state that I am extremely grateful for the consistently up to date and broad knowledge you share monthly with us. I look forward to your columns monthly.

In regards to the recent article in the March 1992 issue of Audubon, I agree it is unfortunate that (the author) Mr. Derr does not consider publication in an aquarium journal valid proof of anything. However, I wonder if this lack of credibility is due in part to a lack of participation by marine reef Hobbyists in the reporting of reproductive events in our tanks. Should we consider this challenge a call to arms and report more vigorously? Perhaps FAMA should start a new monthly column dedicated solely to the reproduction of marine reef specimens by aquarists. This could include reports on all reef inhabitants including true and false corals, crustaceans, coelenterates, mollusks, etc.

As an example, 8 months ago the false coral green disc anemone *Actinodiscus* reproduced in my reef tank. I recorded all tank parameters at that time as well as my observations of the event. Although this apparently is not unusual according to Peter Wilkens in his book, Invertebrates- Stone and False Corals, Colonial Anemones, how many beginner readers of FAMA know that? Would a monthly column on breeding /reproduction in reef tanks stimulate more interest and research as well as reporting by hobbyists? I think so.

It is unfortunate Mr. Derr does not consider Aquarium journals valid avenues of scientific data because I certainly do. I have a Bachelor of Science degree with honors in biology. I also am a physician and have published many articles in the major medical journals in my field. I have kept marine invertebrate tanks for 14 years. I have kept freshwater tanks for over 30 years. I have been regularly scuba diving with particular attention to reef life for 17 years. Despite this, I consider myself simply a moderate to advanced reef aquarium enthusiast and I've learned most of what I know from Aquarium journals in addition to many standard marine aquarium texts. Do you think Mr. Derr would be more impressed if people like myself started reporting nd included all our credentials at the end of the article? I hope not because I am sure there are a lot of hobbyists with perhaps little or no experience in anything else but who are at the cutting edge of marine reef keeping and could contribute a lot to our hobby/science as well as to the preservation of wild reefs through the home propagation of aquarium specimen.

Thanks again for sharing your expertise with us regularly and I look forward to your reply.

Sincerely, Adam F. Petras, San Rafael, CA

A. Thanks for your comments, Adam. You must understand that Mark Derr is just an author, and that his opinions do not necessarily reflect those of the Audubon Society. His article did create a stir in our industry, and I hope that the result is a move in a positive direction. I think his intent was not to improve our industry but to bury it. Many industry people would prefer to see the controversy just settle back down to business as usual, but many hobbyists and industry people perceive that the opportunity is now to re-examine our industry and take steps to make it a better one. This is to everyone's advantage in the long run.

I really don't see a shortage of articles demonstrating success with growing and propagating reef invertebrates. I agree it wouldn't hurt to see more of these articles, and I think that the articles will come naturally as more hobbyists become involved in reef keeping and creating captive ecosystems.

Mr. Derr's suggestion was to publish our findings in scientific and popular journals... I will follow his suggestion, since I think he has a good point. It is true that scientists are barely aware of what the aquarium hobby has achieved. Although I don't believe it is the responsibility of hobbyists to inform scientists about success with growing and reproducing reef invertebrates, it certainly doesn't hurt to do so.

I also agree with your point, Adam, that many "cutting edge" reef keepers have no scientific training at all. These non scientists tend to have the best tanks. "Expertise" with captive ecosystems develops through a combination of an innate "feel" for the environment, an empathy for the inhabitants, with knowledge of their life history that can easily be obtained by reading books. This "empathy" of sorts is the thing that strict science lacks.

A new monthly column is not necessary, but if hobbyists wish to report their success, and they bother to make the effort to use the right photographic equipment to document the event, then I'm sure that this magazine could publish records of spawning and reproduction of marinelife. All too often hobbyists neglect to photograph what has happened, or they take photos which could easily be mistaken for the loch ness monster on the cover of the National Enquirer. Photographic proof surely boosts credibility, particularly when the pictures are sharp.

By the way, Mike Paletta (a.k.a. Richard) had an interesting article on coral propagation in a recent issue of Seascope, and I understand that he has more articles on that subject coming soon in Aquarium Fish Magazine.

Q. Dear Julian,
I have a question about the automatic addition of Kalkwasser. The problem I'm having is trying to understand the shifting reaction from right to left, described by Alf Jacob Nilsen in the FAMA Nov. 90 issue. The reactor uses a magnetic spinner at the base to mix the calcium hydroxide in order to delay the reaction. Will a power head serve the same? If so, how long is the reaction delayed in a 5 gallon reactor? After each reaction shift, will it need removal and cleaning of the powder left at the bottom of the reactor? Where would I locate the inlet tube of the supply line leading calcareous water to the sump? -- top, midway, or lower part of the reactor? As soon as I have a good understanding on the subject, I'm planning to build my own. The reactor will have a direct supply of R.O. water, controlled by a float valve. Mixture from the reactor will be gravity fed to the sump, controlled by another float valve in the sump, replenishing evaporated water. Sincerely, Horacio Rocha, New Bedford, Massachusetts

A. The idea is to keep as much calcium in solution as possible. The calcium tends to react with dissolved CO_2 in the water to form calcium carbonate, which is insoluble and falls out of solution, causing a drop in the concentration of calcium in the Kalkwasser. Since Calcium hydroxide is only slightly soluble, any excess tends to settle on the bottom along with the insoluble calcium carbonate that precipitates out. By stirring the vessel, the undissolved calcium hydroxide is re-suspended which maintains the solution at saturation until enough has reacted with CO_2 so that no more undissolved calcium hydroxide remains, leaving only particulate calcium carbonate and a less than saturated solution of calcium hydroxide. At that point more calcium hydroxide needs to be added. Use of an airstone to stir the kalkwasser is counterproductive since it introduces CO_2 which forms calcium carbonate, resulting in low quality kalkwasser. A powerhead may be used, but in time it will jam up from caked-on calcium. If the powerhead is serviced frequently, then its use is ok. A lid on the reactor will limit the availability of CO_2 and thus slow the degradation of the solution. It is not necessary to get crazy calculating the precise point of saturation. Just remember that about a teaspoon of calcium hydroxide will dissolve in a gallon of fresh water, figure out how many gallons evaporate per day or per week, and add enough calcium hydroxide plus a little excess to your reactor chamber to cover what's lost to precipitation. Don't go nuts please.

Yes, it is desirable to periodically drain out the accumulated undissolved calcium carbonate powder from the bottom of the calcium reactor. You should keep this in mind when designing your reactor...a bottom drain which can be "burped" periodically would serve well. According to Alf Nilsen, leaving this powder there resulted in a slightly lower Kh level in his tank.

Look at the drawing in Mr. Nilsen's article to see the position of the inlet for the exit pipe. The exact position is not critical, but it should be at least a few inches off of the bottom.

If you use this design, Mr. Nilsen cautions that the exit pipe must have a hole drilled in it just near the opening that drains into the tank or filter sump. In time the main pipe opening can become clogged by layers of calcium carbonate, and the extra hole prevents a complete blockage which would cause the reactor to spill over.

If, instead of using Nilsen's calcium reactor design, you are using a reservoir with a dosing pump feeding kalkwasser to the tank, it is necessary to periodically clean the pump and feed line as both will become caked with calcium carbonate.

I'm not sure about your supply of R.O. water. Only one level switch is necessary - - one in the sump which would signal that replacement water is needed. This could be used to fire up a dosing pump to send pure R.O. water from another reservoir into the calcium reactor, which drains by gravity, as you noted. A float valve is not necessary in the sump. I would never recommend using a float valve that can demand R.O. water direct from the tap/supply line. Failure of such a set up would ***Murphy's law variation.**   cause a flood, and Murphy* says that failure is inevitable.

Q. Dear Julian,
I'd like to ask you about bioluminescence. On two occasions I have seen sections of my reef light up. The first time I wasn't sure if I really saw it, but the second time was more intense. I woke up at 3:00 am to go to the bathroom, and I checked the tank and was shocked to see it lit up like a starry night sky. Small specks of light were everywhere, and a small quarter sized spot on one of the live rocks looked like fireworks with threads of light going on and off. The lights were not moving so they were not water born. I found one speck on the glass and put a flashlight on it. The only thing I saw was a small isopod (.075") that I have seen before during the day. They look like small centipedes.

Could you please shed some light (pun) on this subject and any experiences with your own tanks.

Tanks for all the help! Douglas Breda, Marlborough, N.H.

A. I thought this question was appropriate considering that I'm writing this column on the fourth of July. Now that you mention it, Douglas, I wonder why more people have not asked me about this. One of the neat things about a reef tank is that different times of day (or night) afford quite different opportunities for observation. Nightime viewing can be done with a flashlight, or under the poster-board glow of blue light, or in complete darkness, as you have done.

There are many animals in our aquaria which light up like fireflies. Most of them are worms, though some crustaceans and echinoderms also glow in the dark. The quarter sized fireworks display you saw could have been either of two possibilities. It might have been a terrebelid worm or a brittle starfish. I recall the first time I ever saw a brittle starfish light up. I would never have believed it was possible, and the intensity and color is truly out of this world. Usually bioluminescent creatures glow a shade of yellow, green, or blue-green. The starfish I saw glows bright blue, with lightning-like intensity and timing. In the ocean and bays, blooms of a type of dinoflagellate called Noctiluca (night-light) causes the water to light up around any disturbances or agitation. Boats leave a glowing wake, as do fishes. Simply waving your hand in the water produces a sparkler effect...very attractive to hungry sharks, mind you. Ctenophores, the comb jellyfish, also light up the water when they are disturbed. Not much is known about the function of these nightime fireworks like you saw...feeding and predator avoidance are some ideas to play with, but I'm sure there are other possibilities.

Q. Dear Julian,
I have a couple of questions that no pet store has yet been able to answer for me. I am a novice marine aquarist who has recently given up because of lack of time and money, however, I do intend to begin again anew when I am rich and bored (whenever that is). I would like to share some of my experiences and, hopefully, get a few questions answered.

I have a 45 gallon high tank. I began it (after one month of running clean) with two damsels (a lemon and a blue devil), a sebae and a Hatian anemone. After a month I was forced to remove the lemon because it dug a territorial pit in the gravel under a piece of coral and was interfering with the undergravel filter. Is there a way to stop that from happening without removing the filter or the fish?

I checked the water regularly and did a 1/3 water change once a month. The sebae died from a bacterial infection. My anemone was the next to go. I noticed that it had these strange brown brown hairlike things growing from its body. I thought that it was some kind of parasite so I called my dealer who told me that anemones don't get parasites, but he had no idea what it could be. Well, I recently discovered in the May issue of FAMA that they are called acontia filaments and are a sign of stress. Could you elaborate on this?

Finally, my prized, beautiful , 41/2 inch blue devil fell victim to my careless overfeeding.

I started over with a new day actinic light and an extra power filter. I bought a long tentacle anemone, a black sebae, a sailfin tang and a scrawled cowfish.
I fed the long tentacle anemone liquid food. A month or so later, the walls of my tank and everything in it except for the fish was covered with a purple fungus. Of course I called the dealer who informed me that the fungus was a result of too much dissolved organics in the water and that the probable cause was the liquid food. But many of my friends tell me that they use liquid food too and have never had that problem. I could not remove the fungus. It would just grow back by the next week so I was forced to break it down again. Is there something I can use to kill this fungus? I have tried using Maracyn to no avail. Sincerely, Julie Brady, Arlington, VA

A. You are a funny person, Julie, but I'll offer the serious advice you need. I don't know why you ran the tank clean for a month... was this advised to you? The slow start with marine aquariums is to allow populations of beneficial bacteria time to develop in the filter media and substrates in the tank. These bacteria only develop when there is sufficient waste for them to decompose and grow on. An unpopulated tank does not go through a nitrogen cycle unless food or inorganic nitrogen sources are added. It is possible that your tank "cycled" only after you added the fish and anemone...especially considering your admitted tendency to overfeed the tank. You indicated regular water testing, but not the results. Did you note any buildup of ammonia or nitrite?

It does sound like your anemone was stressed and emitting acontia filaments. Most likely it was bothered by some parameter of the water, but I cannot accurately guess what that might have been. Acontia are actually digestive filaments, and they are often employed as a means of defense against predators or encroaching invertebrates, but they are also seen when the stress is just environmental, which could include temperature, pH, excess oxygen, ammonia, nitrite, or toxic metals. I suspect that your tank was not thoroughly established with nitrifying bacteria, but I can't be sure.

**Neoglyphidodon*

Your "blue devil" was probably a blue velvet damsel, *Abudefduf?* *oxyodon*. I have never seen a blue devil, *Chrysiptera cyanea*, which was 41/2 inches long. How do you know you overfed it? Did it pop?
Your "purple fungus" problem is common, frustrating, but easy to solve. I have discussed it numerous times in this column, but yours is a special case, as it is not a "reef tank" we are dealing with. First, for your information the slime is a cyanobacteria, aka "blue-green algae". There are numerous algicides and antibiotic substances which can be employed to eradicate the purple plague, but I prefer to solve the problem by eliminating the pollution which causes it in the first place.

Your dealer was right about the liquid food, and so were your friends. Too much will pollute the tank and stimulate these algae plagues. These foods should only be used sparingly, and are best applied directly over the invertebrate they are intended for. Clownfish anemones get their nutrition from photosynthetic products from their symbiotic zooxanthellae primarily. They take in ammonia and nitrate from the water (or from the clownfish excretions) as food for the zooxanthellae. An occasional piece of shrimp or fish will enhance their growth but is not even necessary. Liquid micro-particle suspensions are not required by the anemones either, but may benefit other invertebrates such as gorgonians.

The use of protein skimming combined with restricted food inputs would soon solve the purple problem. In a reef tank the plague can be more persistent because nutrients which fuel it can be trapped by the rockwork. The skimmer should be sized to filter at least one tank volume per hour, preferably more.

Good luck on your plans for getting rich- hey maybe you could farm the purple stuff. Have you heard about Spirulina? People are making money growing that slime algae and packaging it for the health-conscious consumer.

November 1992   I've got foam on my mind...

Q. Dear Julian,
I've been in the marine hobby for about four years, and I've been quite successful at maintaining a 55 gal. reef tank for two years. I just recently purchased a 125 gal. tank. I plan on using a wet/dry filter made for a 150 gal. tank, with two towers and a 40 gal. tank as a sump. I would like to transfer everything in my 55 gal. to my 125 gal. tank. My question is what is the safest way to transfer everything? I know I will need to buy more live rock, and let the tank cycle. I could even transfer my bio-balls full of bacteria. Where do I go from there?
Thank you for your time. Donald Miller, Phila. PA

A. I recommend that you set up the 125 gallon tank without the bio-towers, just using the 40 gallon sump. Purchase your live rock and place it in the 125 gallon tank with circulating seawater. Allow this system to just run for about three weeks, adding freshwater to make up for evaporation as needed. There is no need for lighting during this period; I recommend leaving the lights off. Light inhibits the development of the populations of bacteria which are growing on the rocks and digesting fouling matter. Light also stimulates the growth of algae which may grow explosively because of excess nutrients from the fouling rock.

You didn't mention a protein skimmer for your set up. You should have one or more skimmers on your 125 gallon tank, and they should be able to process at least 125 gallons per hour.

After about three weeks to a month, if the water in your 125 gallon tank measures no ammonia or nitrite, and no fouling or sulfur smell is evident, it is safe to transfer the contents of your old tank to the new one. If you wish to continue using the biofilter you may transfer it at the same time. When the transfer is made, the lights may be turned on. Remember to keep the photoperiod at ten to twelve hours- not longer. Don't skimp on the skimmer... it is no accessory, for a reef tank with live stony corals it is more important than the biofilter.

Q. Dear Julian,
I have been reading your column for a few months and I have decided to start a saltwater aquarium and all is going well, but I have a few questions for you. First, the problem is that it is a 55 gallon which has a single strip light with two 20watt fluorescent bulbs. At this time I am thinking of adding some invertebrates, but all of the books I've read have been vague about lighting, saying mostly it was a matter of preference which to choose. So I would like to know what you would recommend for all of us novices who might be in the same dilemma. Second, do protein skimmers remove the trace elements from the water. If so, what do you think of the blocks which dissolve in the water to put the elements back in? Ed Mcdermott, PBG, Florida

A. To properly illuminate a 48 inch long 55 gallon aquarium for photosynthetic invertebrates, you may use fluorescents only, or a combination of metal halide and fluorescents. You can get by with a minimum of four standard 48 inch fluorescent tubes, though six would be better. At least two should be blue tubes. If you can use H.O. or VHO tubes, do so, but remember that these require an 800 milliamp or 1500 milliamp ballast, respectively. Two 48 inch blue tubes and two 175 watt metal halides would also work nicely, and would be quite bright.

I know I have discussed your first question in this column before, and I believe I may have covered the second one, but my memory fails me now*, and your question is one that I see and hear often enough that I suspect I could include it in my column like a mascot for years. Yes, protein skimmers remove trace elements. This is not a reason to avoid using them. Here is my argument. Elegance coral removes trace elements. So do leather corals, mushroom anemones, and every other spineless piece of the reef we keep. You have to ask yourself what it is exactly that you wish to keep. A tank just full of seawater with trace elements? --or a thriving, growing coral reef ecosystem? A protein skimmer makes it easy to do the latter feat, at the expense of some trace elements which are easily replenished. Get the picture? There are many trace element replenishing products on the market. I have not tried using the blocks that you mention, but I have heard good things about them from people who use them.

Q. Dear Julian,

I have no experience with aquariums, saltwater or freshwater, but I believe that with enough patience, study and desire to succeed and see the beauty of a thriving aquarium, it can be done. I am planning on setting up a reef tank, but not for another half year or so. Already I've been reading and talking to dealers for six months. I've found that *FAMA* is by far the most informative publication and I'm looking for back issues. I only just found out about the Bucks County Aquarium Society here. Imagine how I feel knowing that I could have spoken to you personally only a few weeks ago!

I am fascinated by anemones and the tank which I am planning will have no more than two fish. I have not bought anything yet. The tank I am planning to use is a pentagonal tank, 44 gallon capacity, and 25 inches deep. I've been told that for fish it would not be good, but for invertebrates it would be fine. The only place I have for a tank is in a corner, away from the direct sunlight by the windows.

I have yet to decide which anemones to keep. I definitely want a shrimp. Probably a scarlet cleaner, a flame scallop, a starfish, but I'm undecided on what else. I've read in your column about starfish compatibility.

The biggest question I have is about lighting. I've heard the pros and cons about all kinds of lighting (some from reef-keeping books, some from advertisers). I've heard that metal halide produces much heat and uses much energy. I've heard that VHO lights lose their spectral quality rapidly, around four months or so. I've read that blue actinic lighting only helps one type of pigment around 420 nanometers and gives an unnatural look to the tank (I am assuming the author meant that this was if actinic lighting was used without daylight tubes). And I've heard that regular fluorescents are not strong enough.

For my tank specifications and the needs of invertebrates, which type of lighting is best? How strong should the lighting be? Also, is it necessary to have a hood or cover? With such an odd shape to the tank I don't know how to cover it, and the hood available will not have the capacity for my lighting.

One last question: does an invertebrate tank have a biological capacity as the fish rule (i.e. five gallons of water for every two inches of fish)?

I appreciate any information you can give me and I look forward to you speaking again at the Bucks County Aquarium Society, hopefully soon.

Sincerely William Schaffner, Croydon, PA

A. My goodness, your determination is admirable. I don't recommend Flame Scallops unless you don't mind that they only last around six months to a year*, and periodically they go mad and flit all over the tank bumping into things. They are really beautiful and worthy of display, but not really for the stable community. Review what I said about starfish. Avoid the chocolate chip star with anemones. A blue *Linkia* star would be fine.

Lighting for your tank is simple. The dimensions of your

*My experience with Flame Scallops has improved over the years. They can survive for much longer periods and they do grow now. This improvement relates to better maintenance of the calcium and alkalinity, and to the more complete ecosystems we maintain now with live sand and live rock.

tank virtually require that you use a metal halide lamp, which may be combined with two blue fluorescents for appearance and benefit to your photosynthetic inverts. I recommend you use a single 175 watt globe metal halide with daylight color temperature, or any of the other daylight spectrum metal halide types, (HQI, or the new compact 6500 K lamp). You may use a hanging pendant fixture and mount the blue tubes separately, or use a fixture that incorporates the metal halide and blue tubes all together. This option also would hang above the tank, leaving it open at the top for easy access. It is not necessary to have a cover. You can build a trim around the top to provide a height barrier to potential jumpers.

Your tank is less than 24 inches wide in all but one diameter, which means that 24 inch bulbs would not work in a canopy. Even if they did fit, they would hardly provide enough light to the bottom of a 25 inch tall tank. Fluorescents alone on your tank, because it is so short in length, would only provide enough light at the top. If your tank was at least 48 inches long, you could provide enough light with fluorescents alone, and the choice would be yours. Regarding heat, a lot of that will build up in a closed canopy, even with a muffin fan. An open tank with hanging fixture will operate cooler than one with a closed canopy.

Your concerns about excessive electricity usage by the metal halide are unfounded. VHO bulbs should be replaced about every six months, but are acceptable for one year. Metal Halide bulbs should be replaced once per year also. Actinic light provides very important energy for the zooxanthellae's photosynthesis. If you ever go scuba diving and observe a coral reef at about 50 feet deep or more, you will note that the light is indeed very much like actinic light, a bit bluer, but the effect is the same, and the corals glow with bright greens, reds, and oranges just like under actinic light---hardly an unnatural look. If you are using a metal halide you do not have to have supplemental blue light, but I think the tank looks nicer when it is used, and I like the effect of twilight when the daylight tubes or metal halide is off, and the tank glows like a psychedelic poster. Such twilight also stimulates fish to spawn.

Photosynthetic invertebrates do not pollute the water in the same manner as fish. In fact, they filter the water, purifying it even of the fishes nitrogenous wastes. However, soft corals emit potent terpenoid compounds which are toxic to stony corals, and stony corals shed mucous and "nettles" which harm soft corals. A protein skimmer will remove much of this biological warfare pollution, but there are limits to how many inverts you can cram into a tank, especially with regard to the physical space and the invertebrates habit of killing each other when they touch.

Suffice it to say that you can densely "plant" the tank with photosynthetic invertebrates, but be sure to provide sufficient room for expansion, and use a good protein skimmer.

Q. Dear Julian,
Your articles are very informative, but now I'm going to tell you my problems. I have a 60 gallon tank with a wet/dry filter system built inside the tank, much like a back hanger. I have metal halide lighting with one actinic 03 and one Bio-Lume fluorescent tube (40 watt) to give my tank what I thought was a full spectrum of lighting. From the sump of my wet/dry filter, I have a Rainbow Lifeguard chemical and mechanical module powered by a "quiet-one" pump that goes through an AFC-2 chiller and then back into the tank. The tank has been established for about two years. I have about 60 lbs of live rock inside the tank. Within the past week, I have lost a curlique anemone and a coral banded shrimp, both of which I have had well over a year. Just before my shrimp died, he had red algae all over him. My dwarf anemone looks ill, and my green star polyp doesn't come out hardly at all. Within the past month, a friend encouraged me to get rid of my brown sailfin tang so that I might get some good algae growth, which I had almost none of. Now I have large crops of hair algae, and it has even grown over my star polyp, which I keep somewhat harvested to help it recover. I also have scattered red algae here and there (which looks horrible). The temperature in the tank is maintained at 77 degrees.

I am using polyfilters, Chemi-zorb carbon, Marine Clarifier by Coralife, Reef Calcium by Seachem, Reef Plus by Seachem, Reef builder and Marine buffer by Seachem. I register no phosphates on tests, Oxygen is between 8 and 9 ppm, Nitrates at zero, and pH at 8.3. I use purified de-ionized water for all water changes and evaporated water loss. Do I want all that algae in my tank or do I need another tang to crop it back. What do I do? Try as i might, I can't seem to get it right. I believe in keeping a suitable environment versus just replacing animals as they die. The little bit of macro algae that I do have is being covered by red algae. I do a 10 gallon water change monthly. Please give me recommendations from where I stand and a possible selection of animals that might help my problem. I have heard that soft corals use up the same nutrients that hair algae uses, which might help the problem. A year ago, when I got my star polyp, he grew so fast and grew right onto the rock I set him on. Then in the past three months his green color went to almost white, and now I'm going frantic trying to keep him alive. As it stands, all I have is a terrible looking tank with an ill dwarf anemone and a black-headed goby that has the run of the tank. Sincerely, John Heins, Twenty Palms, CA.

A. You sound pretty miserable, John, but your troubles can be fixed. You need a protein skimmer, guy, which should be no surprise to hear this month since that is the theme of the letters I have selected. Don't skimp! Build or buy a large and efficient skimmer, and your tank will be on the road to recovery.

Some other changes are in order as well. While canister filters and cartridges are fine for fish tanks, I don't recommend them for reef tanks because reef tanks produce so much detritus, and cartridges trap the dirt and allow it to be broken down, which pollutes the water. Mechanical filters on reef tanks should be changed or cleaned often, which means they should be easily accessible. I would put the tang back, and once he grazes the turfs down a bit, I recommend that you add some Turbo or Astraea snails as well. I use as many as one Astraea snail per gallon, since they are relatively small. Turbo snails are larger, so fewer are needed. It is best to combine the two types. I don't recommend that you add any soft or hard corals until you get the algae problem under control.

I recommend that you lower the temperature to about 74 degrees. I also suspect that your tank does not have strong circulation. Add a powerhead or two to help increase the velocity of tank currents. Your anemone will appreciate this. I'm not sure why your shrimp died. Sometimes algae blooms are toxic, and this may have been the cause, but it is hard to be certain. Did he die from molting? Perhaps there is an iodine deficiency in your tank. Shrimp need iodine to molt properly.

Finally, be sure that your calcium level is at least 400 ppm by adding kalkwasser daily with a drip or dosing system, and be sure to add a Strontium solution as well. I have a suggestion for the star polyp. Use a wooden toothpick to remove the hair algae by inserting it into the mass and twirling it. Once you have removed the bulk of the algae, put a few herbivorous snails on the starpolyp. These will polish off the remaining algae. Please make all of the recommended changes I just offered you, if you want to achieve the satisfaction with your tank that you really hope for.

Thanks for all of your letters, folks--

Notes

Notes

Notes

You should be able to find this book in your local library, book store, aquarium shop, pet store, or public aquarium. If you cannot find it locally, please send a self addressed stamped envelope to:

Ricordea Publishing Inc.,
c/o Two Little Fishies, Inc.,
4016 El Prado Blvd.,
Coconut Grove, Florida, USA, 33133,
Tel (305) 661-7742,
Fax (305) 661-0611,
1-(800) 969-7742
Hours 10 AM to 6 PM Eastern Standard Time, Monday thru Friday.